"It is crucial for us to ponder Carolyn Baker's profound and indispensable exposé of industrial civilization's future. Her words are powerful and her wisdom rich and supportive. We need to seriously reflect on her message if we are to midwife a spiritual vision of life based on compassion, justice, and solidarity."

— Chris Saade, author of
Second Wave Spirituality: Passion for Peace, Passion for Justice

"Carolyn Baker is an outstanding guide to sustaining and even enhancing our emotional and spiritual vitality as we navigate the disintegration of the world as we've known it."

—Bill Plotkin, author of *Soulcraft*

"*Collapsing Consciously: Transformative Truths for Turbulent Times* is one of those books that is not meant to gather dust. It is a book you will want to keep close—in your glove box or in your pocket. Within a year you will see it get dog-eared, and it will become one of your best friends and companions as we all share and experience the shift into a new era of existence."

—Michael Ruppert, author of *Confronting Collapse*

"With this collection of essays and words of true wisdom, Carolyn Baker shows that she is truly one of the very best ports in the impending storm."

—Keith Farnish, author of *Time's Up*

"Kudos, Carolyn Baker! De-riddling paradoxes, lighting up convergences, you walk with the Shadows through the Valley of Jung, to show how kindred spirits working together may evolve a better, saner, more healthful world out of the madness and detritus that envelop us now."

—Gary Corseri, author of *Holy Grail, Holy Grail*

Also available: *Collapsing Consciously Meditations,* an ebook containing additional meditations.

Collapsing
Consciously

Also by Carolyn Baker

Reclaiming the Dark Feminine: The Price of Desire

The Journey of Forgiveness: Fulfilling the Healing Process

U.S. History Uncensored:
What Your High School Textbook Didn't Tell You

Coming Out of Fundamentalist Christianity:
An Autobiography Affirming Sensuality, Social Justice, and the Sacred

Sacred Demise:
Walking the Spiritual Path of Industrial Civilization's Collapse

Navigating the Coming Chaos: A Handbook for Inner Transition

Collapsing Consciously

Transformative Truths for Turbulent Times

CAROLYN BAKER, PHD

FOREWORD BY John Michael Greer

North Atlantic Books
Berkeley, California

Published by
North Atlantic Books
P.O. Box 12327
Berkeley, California 94712

Cover art © iStockphoto.com/ImagineGolf
Cover and book design by Mary Ann Casler
Printed in the United States of America

The poem "Constant," which appears on page 172, is reprinted by permission from Rebecca del Rio.

Collapsing Consciously: Transformative Truths for Turbulent Times is sponsored by the Society for the Study of Native Arts and Sciences, a nonprofit educational corporation whose goals are to develop an educational and cross-cultural perspective linking various scientific, social, and artistic fields; to nurture a holistic view of arts, sciences, humanities, and healing; and to publish and distribute literature on the relationship of mind, body, and nature.

North Atlantic Books' publications are available through most bookstores. For further information, visit our website at www.northatlanticbooks.com or call 800-733-3000.

Library of Congress Cataloging-in-Publication Data

Baker, Carolyn, 1945–
Collapsing consciously : transformative truths for turbulent times / Carolyn Baker, PhD.
        pages cm
Summary: "A collection of 17 meditative essays and 52 weekly reflections, this book is for readers who are concerned about the daunting future humankind has created and who seek inspiration, wisdom, and spiritual purpose in the face of the collapse of industrial civilization"—Provided by publisher.
ISBN 978-1-58394-712-8
1. Mind and body. 2. Conduct of life. I. Title.
BF151.B35 2013

158—dc23   2013006205

1 2 3 4 5 6 7 8 9 Sheridan 18 17 16 15 14 13

Printed on recycled paper

To my father, Dean Baker . . . with gratitude for life
and the promise of consciousness for all beings

Contents

Part 2: Transformative Truths for Turbulent Times 111

Foreword

A Guide for the Journey

There was a time when most people living in industrial nations thought that the big questions had been answered once and for all. If nature still kept a few of her secrets hidden from the prying eyes of scientists, she would, sooner or later, be forced to hand them over; if people in the world's less privileged countries still sweated under the burdens of poverty and ignorance, foreign-aid programs and the unstoppable engines of economic development would, in time, bring them into the modern era; if discrimination still pressed down on the lives and hopes of the urban poor, the onward march of social progress would find a cure in due time. Utopia hadn't quite arrived yet, but people across the industrial world thought they knew what it looked like—and what it looked like was the world they saw around them, with the last few problems neatly filed off.

The splintering of that comfortable consensus has given the last half-dozen decades their central theme. When neoconservative pundit Francis Fukuyama insisted—in a famous 1989 essay, "The End of History?"—that history was over and his side had won, it was clear that what had once been an unquestioned faith had already morphed into a partisan polemic. The years since then have seen every detail of the former consensus faced with questions for which there are no easy answers. The peaking of global oil production (signaling the end of the glut of cheap, abundant energy on which our entire civilization is based) and the first serious impacts of climate change are only two of the most inescapable warning signs announcing the failure of business as usual and the coming of a troubled age—an age for which the modern world, for all its self-proclaimed orientation toward the future, has made no meaningful preparations at all.

The most common response to the crises I've just named—by those who have grappled with the issues at all—has been a frantic search for some technological solution that could prop up the existing order of industrial society. From Sarah Palin fans chanting "Drill, baby, drill!" and corporate hucksters pitching hydrofracturing in oil and gas shales to Wall Street and the media straight through to proponents of solar power, wind power, biodiesel, and other supposedly green alternatives, there's no shortage of people insisting that industrial civilization can be kept running on some energy source other than the one that created and sustained it in the first place. The fact that crippling problems of scale and net energy make it impossible for any of the alternatives to fill the gap simply adds to the bitterness of the debates, as partisans of one or another option use problems faced by rival systems as rhetorical ammunition, while ignoring the equivalent difficulties that beset their own favorite option.

The failure of all attempts to find a technological solution for the crisis of industrial society is easy enough to understand, because the crisis isn't a technological problem. It's the inevitable consequence of any attempt to achieve infinite material growth on a finite planet. Industrial civilization's blind pursuit of that foredoomed goal isn't a technological problem either; its tangled roots reach down into the deep places of the human mind and heart, to the realm of the dreams, visions, and unspoken beliefs that shape the surface of consciousness and behavior. That's the territory in which the crisis of our time has its source, and it's also the place where meaningful responses to that crisis must be found—and to that shadowy but crucially important territory, Carolyn Baker is one of the peak oil movement's most capable guides.

It was in 2006 or 2007—around the time that my blog, *The Archdruid Report*, was attracting its first readers—that I first started seeing the occasional essay by Carolyn on the peak oil news blogs I frequented. At a time when the discussion of peak oil was even more rigidly focused on technological solutions than it is now, her essays consistently broke new ground, raising challenging questions about the psychological and personal dimensions of the end of the age of cheap, abundant energy. Her blog posts and books have continued to push the boundaries of the peak oil conversation, exploring the end of the industrial age as a personal and, ultimately, a spiritual reality: a journey of transformation through which all of us alive at this turn of history's wheel must pass, in one way or another.

That sense of a journey—waiting for us, forced upon us, or both at once—runs all through Carolyn's writing, but *Collapsing Consciously* seems to me to embody it even more clearly than most. Her introduction sets the tone, with a discussion of her own journey out of the familiar belief systems of modern American culture, and what follows develops the same wayfaring spirit in a variety of ways. The resulting book, like her earlier works, takes the collective conversation about the de-industrial future further than it has previously gone, pushing past the increasingly sterile debates about peak oil as an abstraction to come to terms with the human realities of loss, awakening, and renewal that accompany every great historical change.

In facing such a transformation—or, to return to the metaphor I suggested above, in embarking on such a journey—a guidebook is essential. Since the journey into the future is one that none of us can make ahead of anyone else, the best guidance comes from those who have looked further down the path than most, those who can report clearly and honestly on what they have been able to see. Carolyn Baker is such an observer, and *Collapsing Consciously* offers one of the best sources of guidance for the journey ahead.

JOHN MICHAEL GREER

The Archdruid Report
http://thearchdruidreport.blogspot.com

# *Introduction*

Winter morning skies in Indiana are, at best, ominous, and at worst, depressing. For a child in elementary school, light barely appears by the time the school bus arrives. On one such morning, as an eight-year-old, I sat with my parents in our living room as they instructed me to open my new white zipper bible and turn to a particular chapter in the book of Revelation. We took turns reading verses from the chapter, after which my father launched into a mini-sermon on the Rapture, or the Second Coming of Christ, the Antichrist, the mark of the Beast, and the Great Tribulation. For the first time in my young life, I learned that Jesus might return at any moment and take the "saved" with him to heaven, leaving all of the "unsaved" here on earth, where all hell would break loose. Those who were left behind would then have one last chance to be "saved," by refusing to receive the Antichrist's "mark of the Beast," but refusal would ensure torture and death for them. All others would be destroyed after a seven-year Tribulation, in which the Antichrist would reign, which would be followed by the return of Jesus. Upon his return, according to the literal interpretation of Revelation, Jesus and the armies of heaven would fight the battle of Armageddon with the Antichrist and his forces, finally defeating him, slaughtering all unbelievers, and establishing the reign of Jesus for a thousand years upon the earth. At the conclusion of that millennium, Jesus and his kingdom would then return to heaven and obliterate planet earth.

This particular interpretation of Revelation, known as dispensation-alism, along with other end-time biblical prophesy, erupted in the early-nineteenth century with the inventions of Rev. John Nelson Darby of the Plymouth Brethren Church. In 1909 Cyrus Scofield published a reference bible incorporating the teachings of Darby and others who taught the dispensational perspective. Throughout the twentieth century, a ground-swell of fundamentalist Christians embraced the teachings of Scofield, some of the most notable being Hal Lindsey, author of *The Late Great Planet Earth*, and Tim LaHaye and Jerry B. Jenkins, coauthors of the *Left Behind* apocalyptic fiction series.

As these childhood morning bible studies progressed, my parents painted a grim picture of life on earth in the "last days" or "end times." Until well into my twenties, these scenarios lay in the back of my mind. Eventually I passed through an atheism phase in which I rejected all notions of divinity or a higher power. In 1970 Lindsey's *Late Great Planet Earth* was published and became a bestseller. Whenever any mention of the book was made in my presence, I consistently rolled my eyes or laughed out loud, because in the mid-1960s my parents had sent me to a conference in which Lindsey was a featured speaker, and there he per-petuated and refined the indoctrination I had received from the book of Revelation in my childhood. This was only a few years before I came to adamantly reject all things spiritual.

I became a psychotherapist, and throughout the 1980s and 1990s I refined my career, becoming an avid student of Carl Jung and depth psy-chology. One of many Jungian archetypal works that fascinated me was Edward Edinger's *Archetype of the Apocalypse*, which argues that the book of Revelation is replete with symbols from the personal and collective unconscious that depict the transformation of human consciousness, and it has little to do with external, historical events. After a childhood and adolescence of indoctrination in dispensationalism, the archetypal inter-pretation of Revelation was more than a breath of fresh air.

For a bit more than two decades, my focus remained on the human psyche and personal, individual healing. On the one hand, I was well aware of world events and the influence of culture on the individual, but I continued to hold hope that eventually the United States would elect a president who would transform the country from a nation by and for the wealthy to one in which social justice prevailed.

A turning point in my perspective arrived in late 2000 with the election of George W. Bush and the plethora of questions that surfaced regarding the legitimacy of that outcome. That year I met Mike Ruppert and became a subscriber of his newsletter "From the Wilderness." Immediately after the attacks of September 11, 2001, I began researching that event, and countless questions welled up within me about the official story of the attacks presented by the United States government.

In 2002 I learned of peak oil and began researching the state of a world in which cheap, abundant fossil-fuel energy would no longer be available. Soon I became an occasional writer for "From the Wilderness," while at the same time teaching history and psychology in local community colleges. Additionally, I began to connect the dots between energy depletion and what was becoming a swelling housing bubble in the United States.

Alongside these awarenesses, research on global warming and climate change intrigued me. I started publishing a daily digest of alternative news links, which I sent to friends and anyone who wanted to be on my email list. This eventually burgeoned into a website in 2006. As with the election of 2000, questions surfaced about the legitimacy of 2004's electoral outcome. The Iraq War was in full swing, and a number of veterans found themselves in my history classes. The responses were varied, but by 2006, I began noticing a groundswell of opposition to the war, as the families of many of my blue-collar students, mostly Hispanic, were losing significant numbers of relatives to combat in the Middle East.

By 2007 it seemed that the nation was weary and wary of the Bush administration—a mood greatly exacerbated by the devastation of Hurricane Katrina in 2005 and the administration's dunderhead response to it. Furthermore, in 2007 I began receiving phone calls from desperate friends and relatives in California who were venting their woes about being "underwater" on their mortgages and finding themselves teetering on the precipice of foreclosure.

In that year, a plethora of dots from a cluster of crises began connecting for me. Many alternative news websites began publishing articles about the "three *e*'s," the converging crises of energy, environment, and economics. In 2008 the financial collapse in the United States tanked the stock market and engendered massive unemployment.

By 2009 a larger picture had formulated in my mind. I finally grasped that humanity was not confronting a number of unrelated crises or even a convergence of crises, but the collapse of industrial civilization itself and the bedrock paradigm on which it had been established. My training in depth psychology and my fascination with mythology and indigenous spirituality, which that training had launched, compelled me to explore the emotional and spiritual implications for humanity of a total collapse of a way of life to which it had become accustomed—or perhaps, abjectly addicted.

Thus, in 2008 I began making notes on my insights into the collapse, and that winter I began writing *Sacred Demise: Walking the Spiritual Path of Industrial Civilization's Collapse*. With the success of the book, I was inspired to take its contents further in 2011 with *Navigating the Coming Chaos: A Handbook for Inner Transition*. The sale and circulation of both books has wildly exceeded my expectations, and our predicament has profoundly worsened since my first ah-ha moment of recognizing the collapse of industrial civilization. During this time, I have spoken with countless individuals who have been researching collapse for years— many of them far longer than I have. Overwhelmingly, they have told me that what they most desire is not more material arguing for the reality of collapse but articles, books, and documentaries that offer emotional and spiritual preparation for it. Frankly, I have been astounded by the hunger for meaning, purpose, inspiration, comfort, empathy, and a spiritual perspective that followers of my work articulate to me on a regular basis.

Some readers may be put off by the consistent use of the word *collapse* to describe our predicament. They may argue that I should be using "Transition" or Joanna Macy's term, the "Great Turning." Others may prefer that I use "Long Emergency," coined by peak oil author James Howard Kunstler, or the term in the title of John Michael Greer's book *The Long Descent*. While I do often use these terms as well, and while I believe that, should any of our species survive, we will move through the era of collapse into an era of Transition and Great Turning, our inexorable reality in this moment is one of contraction, decline, and demise. Industrial civilization *is* collapsing. However, that is hardly the end of the story. If I believed it were, I would have not written two books on collapse that elaborately venerate the transformational process that human consciousness is now entering and through which it is likely to evolve—a process that may roughly be described as "collapse," "Transition," and "Great Turning."

As I send this book to publication, I have recently confronted a personal collapse in the form of a health challenge. I have been humbled and constrained by a recurrence of breast cancer. And although my treatment is complete and my prognosis very good, having caught it early and choosing to treat it radically and without moderation, I recognize it as yet another spiritual rite of passage similar to others that I have written about so profusely both in this book and elsewhere.

If we are open to the potential lessons of a life-threatening illness, it may mirror the collapse/Transition/Great Turning saga. The body's formerly efficient management systems collapse. Depending on the severity of the decline, one experiences a transition to a more salutary state of physical functioning, or one departs from physical form altogether. A "Great Turning" of some sort may be required in order to survive and thrive in an enhanced state of physical well-being. This may take the form of dietary or other lifestyle changes, and in many cases, they underscore the futility of our former patterns and the inevitability of physiological collapse if we persevere in ignoring what the body demands. At the same time, such alterations open entirely new vistas of functioning that enhance one's awakeness, vitality, and life purpose. A rebirth of sorts ensues.

Like a life-threatening illness in the microcosm, any collapse demands our full attention and committed focus, not to the exclusion of the lighter aspects of life—moments of conviviality, fun, joy, and play—but alongside them. Every form of collapse is a glaring indicator that what we have been doing is not working and will ultimately lead to extinction. In the macrocosm, an unraveling of an entire civilization and the way of life we have known since birth is a stellar opportunity to practice, as the poet Rumi instructs us, "dying before we die." The ultimate meaning to be discovered in that process is not the finality of death but the rebirth that wants to happen.

Simultaneously, we must consider the past and how we arrived at this juncture of the human story, as well as the future, wherein may lie the transformation for which we so insatiably long. If we do not study the causes of our predicament carefully, we are, in the words of Santayana, condemned to repeat them.

For nearly three decades I have been a student of myth and ritual, immersing myself in the imaginal and archetypal and allowing those to illumine all things literal. Having grown up in a subculture and a home ruled by the literal, I have allowed my adult curiosity to revel in the mysteries, the uncertainties, and the symbolism of life and my experience of it. Thus, I am drawn to the perennial wisdom of the towering giants of poetry, story, art, music, and literature. They never have and never will offer us happy stories with happy endings. Rather, they offer us *life*—in all of its angst, beauty, ire, terror, joy, celebration, ecstasy, and demise. For this reason, I have felt compelled to write a book that exudes all of these, consistently bringing every emotion back to what I call the "deeper Self," as the True North of our experience.

More recently, I have been profoundly influenced by the New Cosmology of Thomas Berry and Brian Swimme, as articulated in books such as Berry's *The Great Work, The Sacred Universe,* and *The Dream of the Earth,* and Swimme's *Hidden Heart of the Cosmos* and his video series *Powers of the Universe* and *The Universe Story: A Celebration of the Unfolding of the Cosmos.* Influenced by the works of Jesuit priest, paleontologist, and geologist Teilhard de Chardin, Berry and Swimme are pioneers in a new movement that integrates science and spirituality and that perceives spirit and matter not as binary but as one. Refreshingly, the New Cosmology offers a perspective of the universe as sacred that, by definition, radically alters our relationship with it.

Why this book and why now? Unarguably, our predicament is more dire than it has ever been. In 2012, as I worked on this book, hundreds of

thousands of acres in my home state of Colorado were burned by wild-fires, and shortly before concluding the book, seventy-two wildfires across the American West were uncontained. A drought more severe than any since the Great Depression engulfed at least one-third of the continental United States, and other droughts afflicted continents around the world. Arctic sea ice is melting at dizzying speeds, and this year we learned that beneath rapidly melting ice sheets in the Antarctic lie four billion tons of methane. Asthma and other respiratory illnesses are reaching epidemic proportions, and cancer rates are skyrocketing. Natural disasters and what we now call "superstorms," such as Hurricane Sandy, proliferate all over the globe.

Meanwhile, Europe is rapidly approaching total financial disaster. The United States is following close behind, and China is currently ex-periencing a dramatic economic slowdown. In fact, some traditional economists are beginning to articulate the previously unthinkable: that economic growth is not only waning, but vanishing permanently.

Lest the reader conclude that I am merely verbalizing yet another ver-sion of fundamentalist Christian apocalyptic dispensationalism, allow me to clarify. As I have written elsewhere, the Greek meaning of *apocalypse* is simply, "the unveiling." Not for one moment do I believe that the world will end or that Jesus will return to earth, rescue his chosen few, and then decimate the planet. I do believe, however, that human beings are well on their way to creating mass extinction events of the earth community and of their own species. The only beings who can reverse that outcome, however, are humans themselves.

What is being unveiled at this moment in history is the abysmal fail-ure of the project and paradigm of industrial civilization. On the one hand, this is a frightening, bleak reality with absolutely heartbreaking implications. Yet on the other hand, it is replete with opportunities for the unprecedented evolution of our species into a caliber of being that finds a replication of the paradigm of industrial civilization on this planet unequivocally unthinkable.

I believe that within this book lie incipient threads of inestimable wis-dom that reach back to the earliest insights of our ancient ancestors who understood what Clarissa Pinkola Estés names the "life/death/life" cycle of existence. All wisdom traditions teach that that which flourishes must wither; that which ascends must descend so that transformation can occur.

In 2010 Mike Ruppert asked me to begin a monthly column for his website, CollapseNet, which would focus on emotional and spiritual preparation. The title of the column was "Collapsing Consciously," and this book begins with selected essays from that column series. They are a foundational preparation for the daily reflections that follow. I am grateful for the opportunity to have offered the column for two years and deeply appreciative of the feedback I received from readers regarding its relevance to their journeys of preparation.

We must steady ourselves and hold each other's hands as we navigate current and future realities, and this is the principal reason for the publication of this book and the accompanying ebook of meditations. Together they offer 365 insightful, affirming, and empowering reflections on the collapse of industrial civilization and provide timeless wisdom for navigating an unraveling milieu in the turbulence of the current moment and beyond. Congruent with my commitment to creating beauty in turbulent times, the wisdom imparted here contains not only prose but mystical and inspirational poetry, gently inviting the reader to venture beyond the linear, rational mind and descend into the richer, pulsating domain of soul.

As with *Sacred Demise* and *Navigating the Coming Chaos*, this book is primarily a study—an invitation to deep contemplation and, hopefully, deep conversation with trusted others in our lives who have embarked on the journey of collapse preparation. It contains a treasure trove of inestimable spiritual gems, with commentary intended to enhance the inherent richness of each nugget of perennial wisdom.

I wish to thank my mother for recognizing my acumen for writing and speaking, and for nurturing those gifts without pressure or condemnation. I acknowledge my mentors and friends, Michael Meade, Malidoma Somé, Sobonfu Somé, Andrew Harvey, Miriam MacGillis, Matthew Fox, Richard Rohr, and Maureen Wild, for being extraordinary truth teachers. Thank you, Kathleen Bradley, Kathleen Byrne, Janis Dolnick, Deborah, Clare, Michael and Lynette, Mike Ruppert, Ellen, Carolyne, Carolyn,

David, and Heidi, for your incredible inspiration and support of my work. Thank you, Margaret, for your editing and for the opportunity to work with you in sharing our vision for this planet. Thank you, Sammy, my best canine friend, for your timely invitations to take breaks while working on this manuscript. Thank you, Great Spirit, for compelling me to write this book with unrestrained passion and urgency.

PART I

*Collapse, Transition,
the Great Turning*

The Joy of Mindful Preparation

L et's face it, preparing logistically or emotionally for the collapse of life as we have known it since arriving on this planet is not supposed to be fun. Certainly there are moments when we joke about it with trusted others as we stock our larder with food, water, medical supplies, and a host of other items we might wish to have stored for the Long Emergency. If we decide to relocate to a more sustainable part of the world, we may experience moments of excitement with family or friends who are accompanying us. And if we are given to dark humor, there is no lack of fuel for that particular fire.

Yet, as we contemplate living in a chaotic world, joy is not the first emotion that leaps to mind. In fact, it is the one emotion that tends to get lost in the shuffle of preparation. We may "agonize as we organize" the logistics of navigating the future in terms of acquiring supplies, finding a sustainable location in which to reside, learning skills that will be necessary in a post-collapse world, building relationships with neighbors and community, planting gardens, raising chickens, or taking permaculture classes.

As you, dear reader, may have discovered by now, however, while all of this requires effort, none of it has to be drudgery. For me and for many of us who have been preparing for some years, the entire endeavor can and, I would suggest, *must* be imbued with joy.

As I dialog with countless conscious individuals engaged in preparing for the Long Emergency, without exception, they tell me that if they could not create joy in their lives and balance preparation with play and creating beauty, they would probably give up, because they would feel so much despair. Each person seems to have a unique way of experiencing joy, but in order for him to persevere, it has become a necessity in his daily routine, not a luxury. One man told me, "I eat some ice cream every night, because it makes me happy." A woman said, "I get silly and goofy with my dogs every day, because doing so brings me invigorating joy that revitalizes me and supports me to engage in another round of preparation."

Whether or not we actively practice a specific technique of mindfulness meditation, we are forced to become mindful in the process of preparing for the collapse of industrial civilization. One cannot be mindless and prepare consciously and intentionally at the same time. Yet even as we try on a plethora of "what if" scenarios in our minds, none of which are particularly pleasant, we can experience joy in preparing to navigate a chaotic world—and, what is more, in the throes of that very chaos, there very well may be moments of joy.

In the chaotic world of the future, thousands of things, experiences, and people that we now take for granted may become inexplicably dear to us, even in a milieu where our only contact with them may be in our memories. In that world, the tremendous losses we are likely to encounter will result in savoring and appreciating incredibly simple experiences and sensations, and doing so is likely to evoke deep feelings of joy.

Dominique Browning, author of *Slow Love: How I Lost My Job, Put on My Pajamas, and Found Happiness,* states that "Slow Love is a way of being mindful, in whatever you are doing. It is a way of being open to the wonder and miracle of this world, falling open to it, and making sure you tap into that every day. It can be as simple as helping someone cross the street, enjoying the last bite of a farm fresh egg before heading to the sink, catching the sound of church bells, and really listening to their music" (Penguin, 2011).

What speaks most audibly to me in Browning's prescription for contentment is that the more we lose in the future, the more crucial it will become to savor what we still have. Consumer society inculcates in us the belief that we are entitled to be happy. After all, it's written in the Declaration of Independence, right? All people are endowed by their Creator with the right of life, liberty, and the pursuit of happiness, yes? Actually, the original word Thomas Jefferson used in the Declaration was "property," not "happiness." Eventually property was replaced with happiness, but even so, colonial America did not perceive itself as entitled to happiness, nor did it perceive happiness as synonymous with accumulating worldly possessions.

A chaotic world will unequivocally test our capacity for experiencing a quality of happiness that I refer to as joy—the ability to access a treasure trove of well-being deep within ourselves that transcends our current conditions, whatever those may be. The end of the world as we have known it will shatter the happiness of many people, but at the same time, it may increase their joy. As author and death-and-dying counselor Stephen Levine notes, "The ironic thing is we have almost no contact with joy because of our obsession with happiness."

No matter how bleak the future may at times become, there will undoubtedly be moments of humor, laughter, and even giddiness. Part of supporting ourselves and our community in the Long Emergency will be creating moments or hours of joy, when and where appropriate. These experiences cannot be contingent on sophisticated technology or even electricity. They will probably need to be simple, ingenious, and heartfelt.

In "(F)unemployment: Make the Best of It," Vermont-based journalist Frank Smecker notes that "With all this (f)unemployment going around, there is now more time to get out in the local community, relocalize, meet new people, foster new relationships, grow food together, find food together, restore land bases, take a break, hop on a bike, go swimming, watch the land come alive with animated life and then, resume community-based work" (Dissident Voice, July 23, 2010).

While there is no "fun" in being without an income, as expenses and debts pile up, Smecker believes, as I do, that employment as we know it will probably not exist a decade from now and that this time of massive unemployment creates space in our lives that allows us to prepare for a future of permanent unemployment.

Gratitude is an attitude of thankfulness and a sense of appreciation for what one has in the moment. It implies two things: relationship and humility. The relationship aspect of gratitude means that when one feels grateful, there is something or someone or some force outside oneself to which one feels in some way indebted, as is obvious when one is grateful to another person for a gift or a kindness. In situations where one feels grateful for fortunate circumstances that don't directly involve another person, one is not grateful *to* anyone or anything but simply glad that things worked out as they did.

Even so, the very emotion or thought of gratitude implies that one is not oneself the origin of what one feels grateful for. I may say that it's "just the way things worked out," but I'm not responsible for "things" working out the way they did. Thus, I'm grateful for a particular turn of events. Nevertheless, a relationship with circumstances is implied, as is the reality that I am not in control of them but rather an observer. Of course, a sociopath like Joseph Stalin, who said, "Gratitude is a sickness suffered by dogs," cannot experience gratitude, because it requires empathy and the ability to appreciate oneself as a participant in the human condition.

Gratitude is a state of mind that inherently recognizes interdependence with the external world, whether it be other humans, nature, the sacred, or a combination of these.

In a time of colossal loss, which I anticipate a chaotic world will entail, gratitude for the ability to survive and to have food, water, shelter, companionship, reasonably good health, and the use of one's limbs and senses will be crucial. I imagine that a "glass half-full" perspective will soon supersede the "glass half-empty" outlook among those who have understood and prepared for the collapse of industrial civilization—especially those who have endeavored to prepare emotionally and spiritually. This has always been true in nations and societies experiencing collapse. In the most dire scenarios, being able to find one small thing every day for which one is grateful enhances resilience and the potential to survive. From the Nazi Holocaust to the collapse of the Soviet Union to genocide in Bosnia or Rwanda, thousands of persecuted and displaced human beings have found solace and inspiration in gratitude.

A Light in Dark Times

Winter Solstice

With apologies to readers who live in the South Pacific or the Caribbean, most of us in the Northern Hemisphere experience, in late December, the maximum darkness and coldness of our regions. We may love winter, may love to play in the snow or on the ice, but we cannot escape the feeling of heaviness that less light and warmth brings. While tragedies obviously occur year-round, somehow they feel more foreboding in winter. Loss of income and the absence of heat or food are especially brutal this time of year. We need only ask our friends in the United Kingdom or in rust-belt states like Michigan, Ohio, and Pennsylvania.

But deeply embedded in nature and its seasons is the principle of paradox. Yes, I speak of it frequently. That's because I believe we in the Western world cannot be reminded too often of its inherent role in our lives, especially in the collapse process. Binary thinking is not only a hallmark of our enculturation but may actually have become etched in the depths of our DNA over time. Black or white, either-or, this way or that way permeate the educational systems of modernity and torment our thinking about and preparation for collapse. When will it happen—in this decade or in the next? Will it be fast or slow? Should I take the lone survivor approach or go live in an ecovillage? Should I stay in my home country or expatriate? The binary questions are endless, and limitless obsession with them is likely to leave us in the same predicament as the proverbial dog chasing its own tail.

If collapse is anything, it is a planetary immersion in the maelstrom of paradox. Unless we understand and honor paradox, we will end up, like all of the mainstream media on earth, asking all of the wrong questions.

The most common feeling reported to me by other collapse-aware individuals is feeling schizophrenic, as they know what they know and walk around in a world that would rather walk barefoot across broken glass than know consciously what it already knows unconsciously about the future.

In his poem "In a Dark Time," Theodore Roethke, who suffered from bipolar disorder, asked, "What is madness but nobility of soul at odds with circumstance?" Think about people you've known who were mentally ill. They probably weren't bad people, but people whose souls were noble, and perhaps because of that very nobility, they could not cope with living in a world far madder than they were. Anyone preparing for collapse invariably, on some occasions, feels mad. How at odds with circumstance we are, and how profoundly crazy-making it feels!

If you've read my book *Sacred Demise,* you know that I believe collapse is bringing about the death of the collective Western, Cartesian mind and of the human ego so that a new species of human and a new paradigm for the earth community can be born and nurtured. But as we learn about and prepare for collapse, a battle commences and intensifies within us. In fact, this conflagration is far beyond feeling schizophrenic.

The moment you sign up to discover the truth about collapse and prepare for it, your human ego begins to die and something *greater* begins growing larger. The two of them begin a struggle that from day to day may leave you feeling crazy, angry, joyful, depressed, terrified, giddy, relieved, paranoid, stupid, guilty, liberated, grateful, despairing, heartbroken, courageous, compassionate, lonely, loved, hated—need I continue?

I believe this is precisely the underlying reason millions of people refuse to look honestly at collapse. The ego under all the "yes-buts" has way too much to lose. In other words, let's just keep the show on the road, pretending that there's nothing greater than my human ego—nothing that's tearing at me to become who I *really* am rather than who I prefer to *think* I am.

So here we are, in the dark time of year, with more darkness around us than we could have imagined and with so little time left to prepare for a tsunami of darkness called "collapse." Where the hell is the light? Well, actually, it's right here, right now. The light is in the fact that you woke up this morning and are able to eat food, drink water, and experience another day. It may be in the work you do or the kind thing your neighbor said to you today or the owl that hoots outside your window. The light is waiting to be felt by you in visions of a new paradigm and a new kind of culture that we all have the capacity to create. I support you in spending a great deal of time and energy pondering, savoring, and feeling that vision in your bones. This is not about inserting your head in the sand—or some other place. By no means would I suggest pondering the vision *instead of* the daily news, but rather alongside it. Let that vision light your way in the darkness; let it keep you warm on long, cold, desolate nights, when you feel "pinned against a sweating wall," as Roethke put it, or when you feel mad with paradoxes that your rational mind has no capacity to resolve. Only by holding the vision alongside the current dark, bone-chilling reality can any of us feel "free in the tearing wind."

Contagion

One of Many Collapse Scenarios

I've long been a fan of movie director Steven Soderbergh, whose 2000 movie *Traffic* riveted me when I was living on the U.S.-Mexican border and was actually witnessing daily what the movie was portraying. Like *Traffic*, the 2011 movie *Contagion* demonstrates Soderbergh's capacity for making a film that is intensely realistic without using artificial accoutrements, such as a dramatic musical score, for initiating massive surges of adrenalin. It was precisely this unvarnished realism that, for me, made *Contagion* a chilling and stunning vignette among many of collapse.

A pig eats a morsel of contaminated food dropped from the mouth of a bat, and the pig ends up in a restaurant in Hong Kong as someone's dinner. That someone happens to be a female Minneapolis executive, who has a fling with a man from Chicago while in Hong Kong. Both contaminated, the two go back to their midwestern cities and spread the contagion there. Ultimately, the disease spreads around the world. From that point forward, *Contagion* rivets the viewer to the unfolding of a catastrophic pandemic that demonstrates every aspect of what collapse is likely to manifest—food shortages, panic, violence, paranoia, and the end of life as civilized human beings have known it.

We know that a global pandemic may well exacerbate the collapse that is incontrovertibly underway and may constitute one of those "cliff events"—sudden catastrophes—that punctuate what would otherwise be a slower process, making it devastatingly acute and terrifying. What was most useful for me in viewing *Contagion* was the realism and logical progression of human behaviors that accompany cliff events. And all the while, I was noticing not only the actions of the characters, but the roller coaster of emotions they were experiencing at the end of their lives as they had known them.

I could only wonder: here are several million traumatized individuals whose lives will never be the same. They are scrounging for food, depending daily on FEMA (Federal Emergency Management Agency) food trucks, unable to find any food in grocery stores, unable to venture outside their homes without masks, limiting their social contact to their immediate families, witnessing thieves invade the homes of neighbors and kill them, arming themselves, suffering from insomnia, and living in a state of abject terror. All of this is equivalent to living in a war zone, and those who survive will continue to live with varying degrees of post-traumatic stress disorder. Should they survive the pandemic and its aftermath, and especially in the throes of the contagion panic, they are going to need far more than food, water, shelter, and their lives returning to some semblance of "normal." Quite frankly, if they haven't developed skills of emotional resiliency, they may as well succumb to the contagion, because the quality of life they will be surviving into may not be worth navigating.

This essay is not meant to be a review of *Contagion,* and many aspects of the movie will not be addressed here. What must be noticed, however, is that most human beings who *do have* the capacity to stare down collapse seem to lack the ability to dig deeper into its myriad emotional and spiritual ramifications, focusing only on physical survival issues. While Maslow's hierarchy of needs is relevant in any collapse scenario, that does not mean that after physiological and safety needs are met, the need for love, belonging, self-esteem, and self-actualization magically vanishes. In fact, those "extraneous" needs may scream even more loudly in the human psyche than in "normal" times.

Questions keep recurring for me. Even as instinctual as physical survival is for the human organism, who really wants to live in a world in which all that matters are physiological needs? What, over time, happens to the psyche when the "lesser" needs in the hierarchy are ignored? What kind of human beings are those who manage to survive but do little or nothing to nurture the soul? What kind of new society are they capable of creating, and how could it differ significantly from the vapid, vacuous, barren inner landscape engendered by industrial civilization? In fact, could not a budding society of emotionally myopic survivalists produce a culture as terrifying and devoid of humanity as Huxley's *Brave New World*?

In "Is America Becoming More Spiritually Poor?" storyteller and mythologist Michael Meade notes, "Sometimes 'it's the economy, stupid' and sometimes it is stupid and foolish and cowardly to pretend that the economy is all that matters. More and more children are growing up in the village of hunger and poverty; more and more young people cannot find a job, much less a career opportunity. Those aren't signs of an economic downturn; they are indications of a loss of grandness and a failure of human courage" (Huffington Post, September 20, 2011).

Northern California psychotherapist Francis Weller, in *Entering the Healing Ground: Grief, Ritual, and the Soul of the World,* speaks of one of the fundamental axioms of tribal culture regarding youth, namely, that every new human being born into the village was perceived as bearing a number of gifts that the community needed. This was, in terms of the village, that person's "spiritual employment." Weller states,

> In our modern culture of hyperactivity and pressured lives, we are seldom asked what it is we carried into the world as a gift for the community. The frequent question is: "What do you do for a living?" Or worse: "How do your earn a living?" I find that question obscene. We have gone from being seen as valuable to the community, a carrier of gifts, to having to earn a living. No one asks: "What is the gift you carry in your soul? What have you brought with you into the heart of the village?" There is persistent grief in our psyches from this absence. We have become *spiritually unemployed* (Wisdom Bridge Press, 2011, 42).

In the next culture, our spiritual employment must be not only attended to but consciously deployed in service of the community. Otherwise, the next culture will not be significantly different from this one.

In my travels, people ask, isn't it going to be really traumatic for people when everything collapses, and they can't make sense of it? While this may seem like a no-brainer to many collapse watchers, the fact is that it repeatedly escapes the attention of both the larger society and a great number of people consciously preparing for collapse, who seem nailed to the first floor of Maslow's hierarchy—who are perfectly willing to do the survival dance but are reluctant or resistant to the *sacred* dance.

Yes, survival needs must be addressed first, but they cannot be separated from psycho-spiritual needs—particularly the need for meaning and purpose. Many studies have revealed that, over time, the lack of meaning erodes the souls of human beings as surely as a lack of food and water erodes the body. Lest the reader assume that I'm making this up, the online *Encyclopedia of Death and Dying* states,

> Spiritual crisis or spiritual emergency is recognized by the American Psychiatric Association as a distinct psychological disorder that involves a person's relationship with a transcendent being or force; it might be accompanied by assumptions related to meaning or purpose in life. The disorder may be accompanied by any combination of the following symptoms, which include feelings of depression, despair, loneliness; loss of energy or chronic exhaustion not linked to a physical disorder; loss of control over one's personal and/or professional life; unusual sensitivity to light, sound, and other environmental factors; anger, frustration, lack of patience; loss of identity, purpose, and meaning; withdrawal from life's everyday routines; feelings of madness and insanity; a sense of abandonment by God; feelings of inadequacy; estrangement from family and friends; loss of attention span, self-confidence, and self-esteem; and frequent bouts of spontaneous crying and weeping (http://www.deathreference.com/Sh-Sy/Spiritual-Crisis.html).

This grim description of symptoms outlines several kinds of behaviors and emotional states we might expect to see proliferating among the psycho-spiritually unprepared as collapse intensifies. And we can be certain they will not be assuaged by massive caches of food, weapons, or an extensive library in an underground bunker.

Those who know cognitively that a *Contagion* scenario is a likely one in the collapse process will not have an easy time coping with it, but they are not as apt to be overwhelmed by it as those who refuse to contemplate it. Yet both groups are susceptible to being emotionally flooded as a result of their vulnerability and the uncertainty of the situation, punctuated by panic, anger, and despair in the society at large. Therefore, it behooves everyone to become familiar with internal resources; to practice skills of self-soothing, deep listening and truth telling with friends and family, and regular journaling; and to have an ongoing, daily stillness practice that provides grounding and centering in the midst of chaos. In addition, while those enduring any kind of global pandemic may not be able to serve the community on a large scale outside their quarantined habitation, people can find creative ways to utilize a repertoire of psycho-spiritual skills to direct their attention outside exclusive preoccupation with their personal circumstances.

My Body, My Life

Some of us may be in varying stages of liberating ourselves from Zombie-ism, but if you are reading this book, you are probably thinking deeply about collapse and have been for some time. Clearly, you are a courageous thinker, because you have opened a book that sugarcoats nothing about our predicament.

While I acknowledge and support our innate ability to think and the fact that, in many cases, our intellect may have literally saved our lives, I also want to notice that people superbly trained for survival cannot rely on mental acumen alone. *They must be present in their bodies and with their emotions.* Ask any mountain climber if what she knows and thinks about will keep her safe thousands of feet above level ground. She will tell you that being present in the body, being supremely attentive to every move, every intuitive hunch, every physical sensation, is nothing less than a matter of life and death.

Industrial civilization could not have flourished without disownment of the human body. The church fathers of antiquity, principally Augustine, believed that the body, its sexual impulses in particular, was an adversary of the divine. In early Christian theology, the body was perceived as a wild animal that needed to be whipped into submission. Because women had menstrual cycles and were capable of giving birth, their bodies were thought to be less pure than male bodies. With male projections of women as descendants of Eve—and therefore temptresses—early

Christian theologians preferred to separate themselves from women, and they began to associate physicality with the feminine. For the most part, "good Christian men" lived in their heads, preoccupying themselves with the study of theology, and because the body was thought to be inferior to the spirit and too often "sexually profligate," some literally whipped their bodies into submission through regular flagellation. Physicality became synonymous with the earth, the feminine, and all things messy and out of control. The mental realm was perceived as heavenly, spiritual, masculine, and orderly.

During the Enlightenment, religious fervor was eclipsed by the writings of philosophers who wished to eliminate all religious dogma and replace it with reason. Thinkers such as Voltaire, Descartes, and Hume deplored the fact that religion had been the principal influence in Western thinking since antiquity, and they endeavored to educate their students in the primacy of the intellect.

We might expect such great minds not to throw the baby out with the bathwater, but in terms of the body, we see little difference in their perception of its importance from that of the early Christian theologians. While these philosophers did not consider the body "evil" or something with which we must contend as we endure our earthly "veil of tears," they seem to have become intoxicated with the superiority of the mind over the body. All problems, they believed, could be solved through reason.

As the Enlightenment was eclipsed by the Industrial Revolution of the eighteenth and nineteenth centuries, reason became increasingly valued, not for its own sake, but in service of "progress." The intellect, it was thought, must not merely linger in amazement of itself but must make itself useful by inventing machines that would yield more comfort and financial security to the higher echelons of society.

The 1970s brought us the movie *Rocky* and perhaps one of the first cultural permissions to cultivate physical fitness since the Olympic Games of ancient Greece. An explosion in gym memberships, jogging, and all things fitness ensued. Over the past forty years, medical research has consistently reinforced the reality of our need for physical exercise alongside balanced nutrition and adequate periods of sleep. A plethora of industries has mushroomed from this twentieth-century fitness renaissance, yet I see little evidence that most individuals in this culture have learned to become present in the body.

It really was not until the explosion of mind-body research in the 1980s that modern humans began exploring the mysteries of the body and the subtle, intimate connection between emotions and physiology. Many researchers discovered the reverence for the body inherent in a number of ancient wisdom traditions. Adherents of those traditions, as well as many indigenous tribes, had never experienced the mind-body split that was so fundamental in Christianity and the Enlightenment.

A central feature of Eastern wisdom traditions is the ability to be present or fully attentive to something or someone. Mind-body researchers in the 1980s began investigating the physiological effects of being fully present in the body through various forms of meditation, biofeedback, yoga, and other techniques. Countless studies confirmed the mind-body connection and called into question a civilization that had been largely occupying the head since antiquity. Modern humans were now being asked to understand, at least intellectually, the necessity of holistic living and change their lifestyles accordingly.

After millennia of emphasis on the mind in Western tradition, however, it is still exceedingly difficult for the inhabitants of industrial civilization, myself included, to fully inhabit the body. The magnetic pull to live only in our heads is so enormous that conscious commitment to becoming present in the body is required. From personal experience, I can affirm that the consequences of living only in my head are dangerous and daunting, not to mention the fact that doing so excludes me from parts of myself that I want and need to develop. On the other hand, I can equally affirm that beginning the journey of becoming present in my body has brought me unimaginable rewards. And I do emphasize that this is a process, not a final event.

But what does it mean to be "present in the body and with the emotions"? And, furthermore, what does any of that have to do with preparing for collapse?

First, being present in the body does not mean working out every day or having sex a lot. Both activities can be done while we are a million miles from actually inhabiting our bodies. In brief, being present in the body means consciously feeling our physical sensations and our emotions, and noticing the places in the body where we feel them. If we are not used to being present in the body, this can feel like a lot of work at first. As we practice this kind of body awareness, however, it becomes second nature to us, and, in fact, we begin to notice when we *don't* feel sensations and emotions in the body. We may begin to notice a rather flat emotional affect or our nervous system feeling exhausted with constant mental processing.

Second, let's return to the analogy of the mountain climber. If she is practicing some mindfulness technique, has been honing her intuition, and has been engaging in other forms of physical activity that foster being present in the body, such as a martial arts practice, she is going to be much more alert and attentive than someone who spends most of his or her time engaged in mental activity only. Her attention is clear and focused—a state much better equipped to deal with the life-and-death procedure of mountain climbing—*and* the life-and-death situations one will invariably encounter in collapse.

Finally, I want to reiterate that living in industrial civilization is inherently traumatizing. While thousands of war veterans among us are suffering from PTSD, I have never met any resident of industrial civilization who doesn't carry some form of trauma in their bodies. Need I remind you, dear reader, that the trauma of collapse *will most certainly* evoke the past trauma you carry in the body, unless you are finding a way to address it?

An Exercise for Becoming Present in the Body

One way to begin the journey is to just simply start working on becoming present in the body. I suggest lying on the floor on your back with no distractions and taking some very long, slow, deep belly breaths. Allow yourself to sink into the floor. Then slowly begin tensing the toes, ankles, and calves of the legs and then releasing the tension and breathing into your toes, ankles, and calves. Just notice the sensations. Feel the aliveness of those parts of your body. That means notice the sensations and the energy flowing through that part of your body. If the mind wanders, gently bring it back to your body. Take your time. Continue with this process slowly up to the thighs, buttocks, and belly. Release the tension, breathe into those parts of the body, and feel the aliveness. Continue up through the chest, upper back, shoulder, and neck. Release the tension, breathe into those areas, and feel the aliveness. Then tense all the facial muscles you can tense. Hold the tension, then release, breathe, and feel the aliveness. Feel your heart beating, your body against the floor. Notice your breath as if flows in and out of the nostrils. Before opening your eyes, take a few moments to notice all the sensations of the body. Notice places where there are aches, pain, soreness. Breathe into them. Notice any images or words that come as you feel the sensations. Then take a couple more slow, deep belly breaths. Very slowly open your eyes and get up very slowly.

It's perfectly fine if you fall asleep during this process. If you don't, that's fine too. I like doing this exercise not only before I fall asleep at night but also in the middle of the day when I've been sitting too long or living in my head too much. In the case of the latter, it brings me fully into my body and provides the balance I need to be present as much in my body as in my head.

It may be helpful to write down what you experienced and do the exercise several times, each time noticing new sensations and awareness. Once is not enough to practice being present in the body. With practice, however, you become used to living in the body and can even be somewhat disoriented when living only in the mind.

For some readers, this exercise may be laughably simple, because you may be doing this sort of thing regularly, or you may be engaged in a body process that takes you much deeper than this exercise. For others, who are less familiar with being present in the body, it may feel strange or inconvenient. If you find yourself saying that the whole notion of doing this is silly and meaningless, that should be a red flag that you aren't spending enough time being present in your body. The next question should be, what am I really afraid I might discover in doing this?

Building emotional resilience in preparation for living in a turbulent world is crucial. One significant aspect of this is understanding trauma and recognizing its effects in our lives. Healing our own trauma prepares us for navigating the trauma of a world in collapse and also equips us to assist others who are traumatized by the changes and losses of an unraveling society. A number of techniques are available, such as Somatic Experiencing, Trauma First Aide, Eye Movement Desensitization and Reprocessing (EMDR), and the Trauma Resource Institute—all of which can easily be accessed online.

This past year the National Geographic television channel has run a series entitled *Doomsday Preppers*. The series has focused on families and individuals in the United States who are preparing for some sort of doomsday scenario, whether caused by economic collapse, solar storms, electromagnetic pulses, or nuclear war. Throughout the series, much has been discussed regarding food storage, but almost no mention has been made about the need for physical fitness and healthy nutrition. In fact, as I watched one notably obese prepper proudly displaying his cache of weapons and giving a guided tour of his underground shipping container, I could only wonder about the quality of his diet and the state of his health and endurance.

Let's face it, yet another deterrent to full presence in the body is the standard diet of industrial civilization, which consists largely of processed and genetically modified foods shipped thousands of miles before landing on our plates. I speak here from my own experience. The possibility of a life-threatening illness this past year caused me to drastically change my diet, eliminating almost all dairy, sugar, and meat. As a result, I have lost a significant amount of weight and feel better than I have since I was in my twenties. I'm exercising regularly and sleeping well.

Preparation for a societal unraveling must occur on every level. We must attend to feeding ourselves; having access to clean and abundant drinking water; getting to know our neighbors; learning a variety of skills; relocating, if necessary, to a more sustainable location; and doing all we can to serve the earth community in this time of descent. The fitness of our bodies, our emotions, and our spirits is not optional, but, rather, it is a necessary aspect of mindful preparation and holistic resilience.

Emotional Resilience
in Turbulent Times
Fukushima, March 2011

In March 2011 I presented a workshop on emotional resilience in Northern California, where residents were profoundly anxious regarding the effects of radiation on the West Coast from the Fukushima disaster. On April 1, a San Francisco–area newspaper, the *Bay Citizen*, reported, "Radiation from Japan rained on Berkeley during recent storms at levels that exceeded drinking water standards by 181 times and has been detected in multiple milk samples, but the U.S. government has still not published any official data on nuclear fallout here from the Fukushima disaster."

In typical American media fashion, out of sight, out of mind. Fewer and fewer stories of radiation realities in and issuing from Japan are being reported. An occasional comment surfaced, usually assuring us that we had nothing to fear. It's all so benign. Apparently, we could now move on to "really important" stories, like Obama's 2012 campaign and the royal wedding.

And yet, whether officially reported or not, Americans and billions of others throughout the world are not only terrified about radiation but about their economic future—an economic future that will be inexorably more ruinous as a result of the Japan tragedy and its economic ripples. By that, I do not mean that people feel mild anxiety about embellishing their stock portfolios. They are frightened about how they are going to feed their families, where they will live after losing their house in foreclosure, where they might find employment in a world where having a full-time job is becoming increasingly rare, how they will access health care without insurance or the money to pay out of pocket, and how they will make ends meet in forced or voluntary retirement.

Obviously, these anxieties are relevant to the world's middle classes— not to teeming masses of human beings living on two dollars or less per day. Ironically, however, it is frequently the case that, for all the suffering of abjectly impoverished human beings, they have seldom known any other standard of living and have learned how to survive on virtually nothing. They hear no reports of nuclear meltdowns, and even if they did, such news would seem insignificant in the face of needing to secure food or water for today—a type of existence that contains its own traumas and yields dramatically short lifespans.

Those living a middle-class existence can comfort themselves only for so long by reflecting on the plight of the destitute in far-off places. Their immediate reality is an anomalous deprivation, a stark loss of the familiar, and the looming reality that things will not get better, but only worse. These losses are unpredictably punctuated with frightening events such as extreme weather, natural disasters, nuclear meltdowns, or the terrifying consequences of a rotting infrastructure, such as pipeline explosions or collapsing bridges. These realities take their toll on the body—sleepless nights, a weakened immune system, moodiness, anger, depression, despair, and, often, suicidal thinking. Whether the trauma is dramatic, such as a 9.0 earthquake in Japan, or whether it slowly grinds on, amid a disquieting sense of the permanent loss of so much that one held dear, the landscapes of countless lives are forever, painfully altered, emotionally littered with the charred shells of once exuberant and robust routines.

"But," you may argue, "I haven't been traumatized. My life is amazingly normal. I'm weathering the collapse of industrial civilization reasonably well and feel profoundly grateful."

Indeed, I celebrate your good fortune, but I must add that no inhabitant of industrial civilization is without trauma, because that paradigm itself is, by definition, traumatizing.

It is only when you understand the extent to which you have been traumatized—even if outside of your awareness—that you can effectively prepare for and, yes, welcome the demise of empire and its ghastly assaults on your soul and the earth community.

In the face of extreme weather events and earth changes, skyrocketing food and energy prices, increasingly dramatic expressions of civil unrest globally, massive unemployment, global economic evisceration of the middle classes, and the proliferation of toxins worldwide—whether from hydraulic fracturing in Pennsylvania or leaking reactors in Japan—we are all in varying states of emotional breakdown and breakthrough. The sands are shifting under the feet of all human beings on this planet. Nothing is as it seems. "Things fall apart," wrote William Butler Yeats, "the center cannot hold."

Call it whatever you like—collapse, Transition, Great Turning. Put a happy face on it or a terrified one, but regardless of how you spin it, regardless of how much you want to feel good about it—and there *is* much to feel good about—the changes are dizzying, sometimes delightful, sometimes devastating. It's an exciting time to be alive, and it's an excruciating time to be alive. Sometimes one feels schizophrenic, sometimes bipolar. But all of that—yes, *all* of that—is traumatizing to the human nervous system, and if we don't recognize that, we're probably hiding out in the "Hurt Locker" of empire.

So how do we not hide out? How do we face our trauma, begin healing it, and protect ourselves—as much as humanly possible—from further wounding, particularly as life becomes even more traumatic?

The Transition movement has provided us with a treasure trove of resources for cultivating logistical resilience in our communities through raising awareness, reskilling, and creating self-sufficient and sustainable communities. Anyone not involved in this kind of logistical preparation is only half-awake, yet many individuals believe that no other preparation is necessary. Might that not, in fact, be one characteristic of trauma? Just as the PTSD-scarred combat veteran insists that all he needs is another good battle to feel better, it may be that the hunger for one more gold or silver coin, one more case of freeze-dried food, one more bucket of barley, one more permaculture class, one more round of emergency-response training is yet another means of avoiding the emotional healing and preparation that every human being needs to do in order to navigate the accelerating unraveling of the world as we have known it.

Ten Ways of Developing Emotional Resilience

1. Understand that industrial civilization is inherently traumatizing. Make a list of the ways it has wounded you and those you care about.

2. If you are involved with a Transition initiative, start or join a heart-and-soul group where the psychology of change (see Rob Hopkins's *The Transition Handbook*) can be discussed in depth and where group members can share feelings about the acceleration of collapse and discuss how they are preparing for it emotionally.

3. Become familiar with your emotional repertoire, how you deal with your emotions—or not. Imagine the kinds of emotions that you and others are likely to feel in an unraveling world. How do you imagine yourself dealing with those emotions? How would you prefer to deal with them?

4. Think about how you need to take care of yourself right now in an increasingly stressful world. What stresses do you need to pull back from? What self-nurturing activities do you need to increase?

5. Who is your support system? If you do not have people in your life with whom you can discuss the present and coming chaos, you are doubly stressed. Find people with whom you can talk about this on a regular basis.

6. What are you doing to create joy in your life? Do you have places in your life where you can have fun—without spending money or without talking about preparation for the future?

7. What are you doing to create beauty? Life may become uglier on many levels, including in the physical environment. How can you infuse more beauty into the world? Use art, music, poetry, dance,

theater, storytelling, and other media to enhance the beauty of your community and your immediate environment.

8. Consider creating a regular poetry-reading salon. People can come together, perhaps monthly, to share poems or stories that express the full range of human emotions. Many communities have found poetry-sharing events to be incredibly rich venues for deepening connections and their own emotional resilience.

9. Spend as much time as possible in nature. Read books and articles on ecopsychology. Take contemplative walks or hikes and intentionally engage in dialog with nature. Margaret Emerson's *Contemplative Hiking* is an excellent guide.

10. Engage at least twice a day in some kind of mindfulness practice, such as meditation, inner listening, journaling, or guided visualization. Still another tool for mindfulness and community deepening is sacred, earth-based rituals, which can be done individually or shared in a group.

It is important to remember that challenging experiences are not necessarily traumatizing experiences. The collapse of industrial civilization will be challenging for those who have been preparing for it; for those who haven't, it will involve massive trauma. The less attached we are to living life as we have known it, and the more open and resilient we are—the more we are utilizing the myriad tools that exist for preparing our emotions, our bodies, and our souls for collapse—the more capacity we create for navigating a formidable future.

I do not assume that a world of increasing crises will be a world devoid of cooperation or community building. In her brilliant 2009 book, *A Paradise Built in Hell: The Extraordinary Communities That Arise in Disaster*, Rebecca Solnit notes that in most natural disasters, human beings, in most cases, unite in a spirit of cooperation to support each other. While I certainly concur with Solnit, I am also well aware that cooperation is not the only response to trauma. Sadly, many will react in terror and express their angst violently. Furthermore, the collapse of industrial civilization is most likely to play out in an irregular, "lumpy" fashion in different locations at different times. How it plays out and over what period of time will dictate how humans respond. One thing is certain: responses will not always be benevolent, caring, and cooperative.

Thus, we must prepare for a very uncertain future by consciously cultivating emotional resilience. This involves both addressing the myriad ways in which we have been traumatized by the current paradigm and training to encounter situations in the future—in a world unraveling—that may be even more emotionally challenging.

Hoping for Happiness
or Metabolizing Meaning?

Many persons have a wrong idea of what constitutes true happiness. It is not attained through self-gratification but through fidelity to a worthy purpose.

HELEN KELLER

We hear much these days, especially in sustainability circles, about the happiness index. Gross National Happiness is a term coined in 1972 by the king of Bhutan. While his definition of societal happiness reflected his belief that material and spiritual values must reinforce each other, the notion of collective and individual happiness has been interpreted quite differently in the United States. In 2010, the *Wall Street Journal* published a happiness index related to satisfaction with career choices. More recently, the movie *Happy* focused on a variety of people around the world who spoke about what happiness meant to them and how they were achieving it. Beyond the United States, Helena Norberg-Hodge's excellent 2011 documentary, *The Economics of Happiness* documented the appalling devastation of people and cultures entrenched in globalization and the transformation that occurs when communities divest economically, politically, emotionally, and spiritually from the globalist paradigm.

But the question remains, what is happiness?

For most twenty-first-century Americans, happiness means having lots of money—or at least enough to pay bills and have some left over to spend. And, oh, do they love to spend! In fact, many people confess that their greatest happiness is derived from shopping. For them, happiness means being able to use fossil fuels and other resources as much and as often as they like, having no constraints on consumption, and never having to worry about doing without anything they happen to want. Invariably, they will defend this perspective by citing the Declaration of Independence, which speaks of the right to "life, liberty, and the pursuit of happiness." Since they usually have little knowledge of U.S. history, they are probably unaware of the fact that in the original draft of the Declaration, Jefferson wrote "life, liberty, and the pursuit of property," which was later changed to "happiness." Yet "happiness" to the American colonists hardly meant what it means to twenty-first-century Americans. Essentially, it meant the ability to live a relatively peaceful life, to provide for one's family, and to pursue one's life work.

Today, Americans are addicted to a particular notion of happiness that is defended by indefatigable "positive thinking"—typified by yellow smiley faces, à la the world's largest corporation, Walmart. In her book *Bright-Sided: How the Relentless Promotion of Positive Thinking Has Undermined America*, Barbara Ehrenreich argues that positive thinking in American culture means believing that the world is shaped by our wants and desires and that if we focus on the good, the bad ceases to exist. Ehrenreich believes this notion has permeated our society and that the refusal to acknowledge that bad things could happen is in some way responsible for the current financial crisis. She, of course, attributes that crisis to many other causative factors as well, but she notes that positive thinking has become an integral aspect of corporate culture. You can't sell things to people or convince them that they can't live without a certain product absent a positive attitude and the subtle message that they "need" a certain lifestyle in order to remain positive about life.

This notion of happiness could not be more divergent from the definition offered by the king of Bhutan in 1972 or the documentary *The Economics of Happiness*. Neither of those is based on the assumption of

America's—or any other nation's—entitlement to "be happy." In fact, as a practicing Buddhist, the king of Bhutan was well aware that the first tenet of his religion is the awareness that suffering is a fundamental aspect of the human condition.

If we examine the etymology of the word *happiness,* we notice that it is related to words like *happen, haphazard,* and *happenstance.* That is because the root word, *hap,* means "fortune" or "chance." Sometimes we are fortunate enough to be happy, and at other times we are, unfortunately, *un*-happy. Presumably, mature adults understand this, but a culture of two-year-olds does not.

I believe that since the end of World War II, positive thinking has become the quasi-religion of industrial civilization, and the failure to maintain it has become tantamount to treason. To be anything but positive is to question the fundamental underpinnings of consumerist, corporate culture. In fact, for nearly a century the Western world has touted the "we can" attitude as the deciding factor in its ascendancy to economic and military supremacy following the Great Depression and the Second World War. More recently, Barack Obama essentially based his presidential campaign on it, and during his administration, we have witnessed the triumph of "we can" in the death of Osama Bin Laden. For a few days, Americans were "happy." Oil prices fell, along with the price of silver and gold, and all was peachy until we saw the ugly jobs report five days later. But wait, it wasn't really ugly, was it? Forget that there had been 474,000 new unemployment claims in one week, so many "new jobs" had been added to the economy. Frantically clawing at the last shreds of "happiness," all of the mainstream media emphasized the "jobs" (of the part-time, burger-flipping, no-benefits variety) that had been created instead of the jaw-dropping reality of another unemployment tsunami.

Meanwhile, back to the king of Bhutan and Helena Norberg-Hodge, both of whom seem to grasp that what matters is not "happiness" but meaning. The happiness of which they speak is not about momentary pleasure or feel-good states of well-being but something far deeper. Happiness comes and goes, but meaning doesn't. The truth, of course, is that we can find meaning in experiences that are anything *but* happy. Very often, when we are unhappy, reflecting on past moments of meaning can elevate our mood to a state of happiness or near-happiness.

However, the purpose of finding meaning is not so that we can use it as a mood elevator. Finding meaning in an experience, a place, an event, a relationship, a task, serves a much broader and deeper purpose, because when something or someone is meaningful, the core of our humanity is amplified. Somehow our lives and experiences make more sense, and interconnected patterns of our life's journey begin to reveal themselves and find their own place. While this may not evoke instant happiness, it may provide a long-term sense of fulfillment. And with that fulfillment may come a sense of joy, which is palpably different from happiness.

Happiness has been sold to us by industrial civilization as a bill of goods that will somehow provide not only meaning but also an identity. Perhaps if we shop enough; look good enough; are successful enough, sexy enough, bright enough, and charismatic enough, we'll manage to find out who we really are. Of course, this unconscious agenda to find meaning and identity, we believe, must be carried out entirely in the light. Ignoring the wisdom of the ages, we pursue happiness (the light) like bored, housebound children on a winter afternoon, believing that the light will make us, at last and eternally, happy. But the light only obscures the one place where meaning is found: the darkness. Or as the author and mystic Peter Kingsley states, "It is impossible to reach the light at the cost of rejecting the darkness."

Ultimately, facing the darkness is all about facing death. The consummate lie of industrial civilization is that somehow, if we consume, consume, consume, if we perfect the human ego while basking in the light, we will outwit death and become eternally invincible. To speak of collapse, peak oil, demise, downturns, economic depression, or unraveling is anathema, because it rattles the rice paper–thin bulwarks we have constructed around darkness and death. This is precisely why often in my workshops I incorporate an ancient Zen Buddhist exercise, which in that tradition, as well as in the writings of Rumi, is known as "die before you die."

The most frequent question I receive from readers is, "I can't talk with my family [spouse, life partner, children] about collapse. They won't listen, and they tell me that I'm crazy. What can I do?" While I have a number of suggestions and, in fact, have created an entire daylong workshop on this issue, the real truth is that people aren't going to be able to come fully to terms with collapse until they "die before they die." Our indigenous ancestors knew this reality intimately, which is why they created initiation ceremonies for their young that invariably involved a brush with death. Again, in the words of Peter Kingsley, "The truth is so simple, so lovingly simple: if we want to grow up, become true men and women, we have to face death before we die."

When participants in my workshops have experienced dying before they die, they are often dramatically liberated to examine and discuss collapse more deeply than ever before. It is as if, once we get dying out of the way, we can move forward and inward to explore its finer nuances and notice how they feel in our bodies. And paradoxically, and almost without exception, I find that when people "die before they die," they report feeling an unprecedented sense of aliveness and vitality.

Perhaps the most rewarding aspect of exploring darkness and death consciously is that doing so invariably deepens all of the textures and flavors of joy in our lives. Joy, a more profound and penetrating emotional state than happiness, is directly related to finding meaning. In a 2011 blog post, British Transitioner Charlotte Du Cann writes about the difference between joy and simply feeling good, "I realized that Transition was more like alchemy than the behavioural change psychologists and social scientists were talking about. And that the first step of alchemy is not enlightenment, but the forcing out of the *material,* the dark stuff you have to transform."

Du Cann succinctly spotlights the profound difference between "happiness" and joy.

> Institutionalised happiness, spin-doctor feel-good, is not joy, or love or merriment, anymore than lifestyle is life, or glamour is beauty. It's a superficial panacea, a coping mechanism, so we don't access and demand our rights for real joy and equity on the planet. So we don't ask ourselves deep questions about why so

many of us are poor and unhappy and why people everywhere are taking to the streets. Real joy kickstarts the kind of alchemy that shifts the base mindset of the world into the high frequency of the heart. This alchemy starts by pressuring the lowest elements down into their base material, forcing the beast out of the matter. Once out of its hiding place, transformation can begin.

Happiness is about being in our heads; joy is about being in our hearts. Joy is the feeling of meaning and deep satisfaction after we have worked for an afternoon in the garden, or at the end of the day, when we and some neighbors have constructed a brand new chicken coop, or when, next winter, we can open a jar of organic fruit that we grew in our garden and canned on a hot summer afternoon with our friends. Joy is what we feel when we can spend an evening with friends and neighbors discussing collapse and how it's changed our lives—the good, the bad, the ugly, and everything in between. Joy is that deep sense of meaning and purpose we feel as we prepare, even as it weaves itself in and out of grief, anger, fear, and despair in our psyches.

Acknowledging and preparing for collapse has little to do with "being happy" but everything to do with creating and sustaining joy. As we allow ourselves to explore the meaning of collapse and our purpose in it, we may be able to gain some salutary distance from its horrors and hold alongside them a sense of joyful fulfillment that surpasses momentary happiness. How do we find meaning in collapse? One way is by asking what collapse wants from us. What does it want us to *be*, as well as do? Even if we never answer the questions as fully as we would like, it may be that answering them is less important than the meaning we metabolize by asking.

It's All about "Down"

It's not the technical dimension of the predicament of industrial society that matters most just now. It's the inner dimension, the murky realm of non-rational factors that keep our civilization from doing anything that doesn't make the situation worse, that must be faced if anything constructive is going to happen at all. In a civilization that's spent the last three and a half centuries trying to pretend that this inner dimension doesn't matter, it was a foregone conclusion that most people's inner lives would end up an unholy mess.

JOHN MICHAEL GREER, "Bringing It Down to Earth"

I have the greatest respect for author and futurist, John Michael Greer. In *The Long Descent* and in *The Ecotechnic Future*, Greer has brilliantly articulated humankind's predicament in the face of energy depletion, economic meltdown, and environmental catastrophe. Yet in "Bringing It Down to Earth," posted on his blog, the Archdruid Report, in 2011, he summarizes the paramount theme of my work: *The technical dimension of our predicament is less important than the inner dimension because until we address the inner, we are doomed to worsen the severity of our situation.*

After more than a decade of awareness about peak oil and libraries of books and documentaries on preparing for it, one researcher who has incisively assessed our plight is now asserting that without a transformation of our inner world, nothing constructive is going to emerge from all of our best attempts to address the daunting issues we are confronting.

Greer is pleading with us to "bring it down to earth"—bring our attention down to the inner world and down into our bodies. It is as if he is beseeching us to drag it to the soles of our feet and feel them nakedly ensconced on the lush, grassy earth. A writer whose style is unmistakably cerebral, Greer shifts his tone a bit in this blog post and confronts us with what is at stake if we continue living in our heads, minimizing our inner preparation. The soul blossoms and flourishes not by going upward but by going down into the depths of emotion, body sensation, and intimate communion with nature.

The demise of industrial civilization is pulling everything downward, and I can only wonder what would happen if, instead of resisting, we surrendered to the downward momentum.

Am I suggesting that collapse is a bottomless pit of dissolution? Absolutely not, but before we can discuss "up," we need to consider "through," because the only way out—and ultimately up—is through.

The so-called Dark Ages, culminating in the horrors of the Black Death, seemed to many human beings a clear indication that humanity was spiraling downward into an oblivion from which it could never recover. Thus, as the medieval era gave way to the Renaissance and then the Enlightenment, humans became obsessed with reason as the ultimate antidote to ignorance, superstition, and blind faith. This obsession continued from the eighteenth century into the twenty-first, and the tectonic plates of this obsession are now rumbling beneath our feet and in our bodies. Humanity reels on the precipice of another dark age—with one important difference. We have the tools to notice what our medieval ancestors could not, namely, that all manner of darkness offers our species an extraordinary opportunity for remaking itself. They were unable to make the pivotal distinction between reason and consciousness, which may be the primary task of our species as we descend once again into horrors of our own making.

Whereas the Age of Enlightenment was lived for and through the mind, the coming Age of Endarkenment will be lived for and through the soul. The *soul* is not a religious term but a notion that runs like a red thread through mythology, indigenous wisdom, multicultural awareness, and human imagination. The best explanation I have heard to date is provided by storyteller and mythologist Michael Meade in his recent book *Fate and Destiny: The Two Agreements of the Soul*. He says that the soul is the "connecting principle of life." It is relational and serves to join opposites—a "subtle go-between that connects unlike things . . . the both/and factor, the unifying third between any opposing force." Moreover, "We are most lost and truly abandoned when we have lost touch with our own soul" (Greenfire Press, 2010).

Likewise, a culture is lost, abandoned, and consigns itself to a trajectory of dissolution when it ignores the soul. For our ancestors, nature and culture were not separate, and where they met, soul was present; soul was the missing element when nature and culture were in conflict. But as the mystical poet Rumi reminds us, "What the material world values does not shine the same in the truth of the soul."

The principal task of Enlightenment thinkers was to exterminate all things "irrational"; any suggestion of soul in humans, in culture, or in nature was anathema to them. I would argue that whereas the paramount agenda of the Enlightenment was to annihilate soul, the paramount task of the Age of Endarkenment (a name coined by author Michael Ventura) will be to reclaim and celebrate our relationship with it. Moreover, this will not occur without enormous suffering, resistance to which will accomplish nothing other than exacerbating the severity of that suffering.

The Enlightenment mind was—and is—obsessed with progress, soaring, and the notion that "every day, in every way, everything is getting better and better." The soul, on the other hand, loves darkness, descent, downward mobility, and the razor-sharp adversities of the human condition. In dark times, it doesn't have to be guided; it knows exactly what to do. In every tragedy, in every gathering of people to mourn loss, soul is there, waiting to be seen and embraced. Remember those myriad memorial altars and gatherings after September 11, 2001? Everyone says that people came together then, and indeed, they did, and that is precisely what soul does in the wake of suffering. It brings us closer to each other, to the earth, to ourselves.

Soul waits like a crouched predator to deepen us, but that can't happen when we're obsessed with the light, with progress, with stuff, with our ego identity. "Deeper?" you may ask, "Deeper into what?" Deeper into our humanity, deeper into our essence, deeper into that which connects all life and all of the earth community.

But things have to get much darker in order for us to get deeper. That is why it is so important at this time not to resist the downward movement but to go with it. You want progress? As Michael Meade reminds us, "Descent is the way the soul progresses." In fact, the act of birth itself is a descent. In ancient times, a woman did not lie down to give birth, but squatted somewhere in nature, and the newborn fell to earth from her body. It is now time for our species to "fall to the earth" once again and become fully present, fully embodied, fully here.

As I have mentioned in other writings, one of the great minds of the Enlightenment was René Descartes, who succinctly articulated the essence of his era, namely, "I think, therefore I am." This from a man who was virtually never held as a child, rejected by his father when his mother died from giving birth to him. Since Descartes, the Enlightenment and its inevitable legacy, industrial civilization, have endeavored to take us far away from our bodies and souls and seduce us into being somewhere else.

But in order to be fully here, we have to descend. The Enlightenment took us "there"; the Endarkenment will compel us to be "here." The Enlightenment doesn't like darkness, but in fact, all creativity, even life itself, comes from darkness and emptiness. So when the darkness descends, a time of extraordinary creativity is available to us.

We stand now at an end/beginning, and as noted above, soul lives and thrives in the territory of opposites. Our job is to hold the opposites of end and beginning as the whole planet experiences collapse. The answers lie not on one side or the other, but in holding the tension of opposites. When a culture falls apart, and when people fall apart, soul centers everything. It does this by compelling us to connect, especially with community and the support of trusted others. It also compels us to create—to create beauty, art, music, poetry, and new ways of being in relationship with all of life. What a fabulous opportunity to make and remake soul and all of its delicious expressions in the world!

Navigating the Age of Endarkenment is not about physical survival, although who would not prefer survival to the alternative—unless the alternative is a fate worse than death? The Enlightenment was all about becoming something other than human—other than what we are. Endarkenment demands that we become intimately connected with the sacred Self within ourselves and all beings. The way out is *through*—not above, under, around, but through. Yet even as we descend and then soar, it is crucial to remember that, at some point, another descent is inevitable. The life/death/life cycle is an inherent law of the soul.

Greer's blog post is asking us to "learn how to get along with the non-rational side of our inner lives." He is vague about how we might do this but suggests general study of psychology, philosophy, religion, and magic, emphasizing that we should pursue whatever in these disciplines appeals to us. All he asks, really, is that we open to the nonrational side of ourselves and allow it to call us to whatever paths resonate. Moreover, says Greer, "The recognition that these two transformations, the outer and the inner, work in parallel and have to be carried out together is the missing piece that the sustainability movements of the Seventies never quite caught." And I would add that a plethora of movements have not caught this piece precisely because they did not deeply examine the binary legacy of the Enlightenment.

The haunting question of the moment is, will we again miss the fundamental integration of the inner and the outer, or will we at last recognize their inextricable correlation?

One of my favorite questions to those who argue against the relevance of the nonrational is, how will you live with yourself as collapse intensifies? I heartily concur with Michael Meade when he asserts, "When a person learns to become who they already are at their core, they find a way to live with themselves in dark times."

Masculine, Feminine, Collapse, and the Next Culture

During the past three years, since the publication of my two books focused on the collapse of industrial civilization, *Sacred Demise: Walking the Spiritual Path of Industrial Civilization's Collapse* and *Navigating the Coming Chaos: A Handbook for Inner Transition,* I have been asked countless times how I predict people of color, women, children, the elderly, and the LGBT community—the most vulnerable members of a society in chaos—will be treated as industrial civilization continues to unravel. Many point to James Howard Kunstler's futuristic novels as one likely scenario. Kunstler essentially believes that, during and after the demise of civilization, minorities will be blatantly scapegoated as a principal cause of the demise and that, as the criminal and legal systems crumble, virtually nothing will deter crazed and criminal elements from foisting all manner of violence on the most defenseless. Kunstler argues that the gains experienced by ethnic minorities, women, and gays in the past forty years will essentially be erased as berserk, belligerent males succeed in ruling the day.

In *Navigating the Coming Chaos,* I wrote very candidly about how I imagine women will be treated as existing societal structures deteriorate. Frankly, I agree with Kunstler that women and minorities will be targeted, and that members of targeted groups who believe otherwise are pathetically naïve. While I have never launched a crusade to arm women, whenever I am asked about how I believe they will be treated in collapse,

43

I implore them to learn self-defense techniques and, if they are open to it, to complete at least one round of training in the use of firearms and to practice using them.

However, to insist that all gains made by targeted groups will be permanently obliterated defies history. Beginning with the plight of ancient Hebraic peoples, slavery was never forgotten, and they carried with them the legacy of liberation from antiquity into the modern world. Africans brought to the Americas in the fifteenth century and thereafter continued to cherish the prospect of freedom and allowed it to profoundly inform the civil rights movement of the 1950s and 1960s. The native peoples of the Americas, who endured generations of genocide and exploitation, have reclaimed and continue to embrace their heritage and significant portions of their traditions in the twentieth and twenty-first centuries. The women's movement of the 1960s and 1970s was engendered by a variety of factors, not the least of which was a knowledge of the history of women and an awareness of their oppression throughout most of recorded human history. So while the powerful can exploit the vulnerable for centuries or millennia, the memory and legacy of freedom and dignity cannot be erased.

Lest anyone infer that I am underestimating the proliferation of evil in a collapsing world, please hear me clearly. I am committed to the work I'm doing—preparing people emotionally and spiritually for the collapse of industrial civilization—*precisely* because of how treacherous I believe the process will be. I do not view the demise as a uniform, systematic occurrence. Circumstances will vary from one community and region to another. I use the word *lumpy* to describe this phenomenon. Sustainability and self-sufficiency may well be pivotal factors in the well-being of individuals and communities as things fall apart, but nothing is certain as to how any person or group will fare in the wake of dwindling energy supplies, resource wars, tipping-point climate change, and worldwide economic meltdown.

In June 2012 there were stories in the news of people cannibalizing other people and dismembering their own bodies and the bodies of others. One man cut open his abdomen and threw pieces of his intestines at police. Supposedly, these acts were done by mentally ill individuals or people under the influence of narcotics. Yet let's notice that we are in the early stages of a society unraveling. If these kinds of bizarre acts are being committed at this stage of collapse, we can only imagine—or not—what kinds of behavior we might witness as what we call a "civilization" continues to deteriorate.

As police departments go away, along with the entire criminal justice system, I anticipate unprecedented escalations of violence. And, I would add, not only against women, ethnic minorities, and the LGBT community, but against white, heterosexual males as well. White males may be the major perpetrators of violence in collapse, but that does not guarantee the safety of any other white male in a treacherous, every-man-for-himself world.

The title of my last book contains the words, "the coming chaos," yet we are already immersed in chaos. I anticipate much more and much worse chaos than we are already witnessing. How bad? You may want to watch the movies *The Road* or *The Book of Eli*. Purely speculative, but poignant food for thought.

For decades I have been profoundly influenced by the work of Carl Jung, Joseph Campbell, Malidoma Somé, Michael Meade, Clarissa Pinkola Estés, and Marion Woodman. Before labeling these people New Age, please read what they have actually written. If you don't understand it, do not write it off as New Age. Know also that I am adamantly opposed to New Age notions, because I know that they have nothing to do with the people I have just mentioned and because the New Age perspective is profoundly, willfully blind to the collapse of industrial civilization. Not only is it steeped in denial, but, in my opinion, it violates the wholeness and integrity of the human soul by insisting that humans are "perfect, flawless, and divine." It denies and minimizes the human shadow, which regularly gets all of us in trouble but also has the capacity to get us in the right *kind* of trouble—the trouble we need in order to navigate the present and coming chaos.

Jung pioneered a new perspective on gender by examining archetypes in the human unconscious. Let me hasten to add that—in case you're thinking that the concept of archetypes is too esoteric, arcane, or antiquated—the director Ridley Scott spoke freely of the archetypes that pervade his 2012 movie, *Prometheus*. Artists and creative individuals are, typically, keenly aware of archetypes and employ them freely in their works. Whereas modern thinkers often scoff at the notion of archetypes, ancient mythology was permeated by them, and much of what we call "modern civilization," while minimizing their importance, has been profoundly influenced by these universal motifs. For example, we need only view organized religions superficially to notice glaring archetypal influences brought forth from antiquity. The same phenomenon can be observed in other institutions, such as finance, education, communications, and health care, to name only a few examples.

Two archetypes that dominate mythology are the *masculine* and the *feminine*. Remember that archetypes are universal themes in the psyche and in art, music, literature, poetry, and drama. Since they are themes, they are different from actual men and women, but both genders are incessantly influenced by them.

The following table may be useful.

GENDER: FROM ARCHETYPE TO INDIVIDUAL

MASCULINE ARCHETYPE	FEMININE ARCHETYPE
Qualities of Masculine	*Qualities of Feminine*
——▶	◀——
Discerning	Intuitive
Protective	Accepting
Reasoning	Feeling
Discriminating	Unifying
Distinction	Relationship
Boundaries	Wholeness
Structure	Beauty
Product	Process
Inferior Function	*Inferior Function*
Anima	Animus
Shadow	Shadow
♂ Individual Man	♀ Individual Woman

In this table we see the classic characteristics of the masculine and feminine archetypes. The two arrows near the top point to the interaction of archetypes from time to time, in which the masculine appreciates so-called feminine qualities, such as beauty, or the feminine employs so-called masculine qualities, such as reasoning.

Extremely significant in Jung's theory of masculine and feminine archetypes, as indicated above, is what he called the "inferior function" of each. The inferior function in the masculine is the *anima,* the feminine principle, and the inferior function in the feminine is the *animus,* the masculine principle. The male psyche carries within it the *anima,* that is, many feminine qualities, and the female psyche carries within it the *animus,* many masculine qualities (both indicated above). In Eastern traditions, the terms *feminine* and *masculine* are referred to as *yin* and *yang,* and spiritual traditions of the East seek to balance both within the individual.

Furthermore, it is important to understand that both masculine and feminine archetypes have what Jung called the *shadow.* That is to say, both archetypes are essentially neutral, neither benevolent nor malevolent, but within the shadow may reside benevolent or malevolent qualities. For example, the masculine holds the capacity for being discerning, discriminating, and making distinctions, but the shadow masculine can express these qualities in a hostile or rejecting manner that marginalizes, excludes, persecutes, or even exterminates others. Similarly, the feminine is a unifying, accepting, relational energy, but without the masculine quality of discernment, the feminine can inappropriately include and accept that which is harmful to her and thereby endanger herself and those she loves.

Finally, at the bottom of the table, we see the individual man and woman, whose complicated psyches are composed of archetypes, *anima,* *animus,* and shadow, and in whose bodies flow hormonal rivers common to both genders.

So how does one prevent living from the masculine or feminine shadow? Quite frankly, by exploring it and knowing what is there. Understanding the shadow masculine or shadow feminine in oneself is crucial not only for enhancing one's own wholeness but for championing justice between genders and all diverse groups in the community. If the shadow is not recognized and dealt with, it will dominate an individual or

. . . community, resulting in untold suffering. Tragically, the shadow in a society may go unrecognized for centuries or longer before being confronted.

In the 1960s women began confronting the shadow masculine that had dominated most societies for millennia. This led to a full-fledged feminist movement, which advanced the status of women to levels unprecedented in the modern world. As is typical of social movements, the participants confronted the shadow of the other but had much more difficulty confronting their own. My very first book, published in 1996, *Reclaiming the Dark Feminine: The Price of Desire*, addresses the failure of feminism in general and women in particular to explore both the shadow feminine and shadow masculine within themselves, and it explores the consequences of that omission.

In the early and mid-1990s, a significant number of men around the world formed men's groups and began exploring the *anima,* which led to a brief but impactful men's movement. Some of these groups still exist and meet regularly, as do women's groups, which, by and large, have moved beyond or broadened the issues with which women were preoccupied in the early days of the feminist movement.

I suspect that in the throes of societies in chaos, involvement with men's and women's groups will be dramatically minimized, but regardless of how tumultuous the upheaval may be, the profound soul-making work that has occurred in these groups will not be extinguished. In fact, men and women may discover that groups focusing on the issues of their own gender are more relevant than ever, because gender issues will become intense as panic, rage, and scapegoating ensue. It is probably safe to assume that significant numbers of people of both genders will become barbaric, and it is anyone's guess as to how long that scenario will extend into the future.

At some point, however, those who would forge the next culture—one in which justice, human dignity, and compassion prevail, one that is not merely another version of the industrial civilization paradigm—will need to possess some memory of the struggles between genders in the past culture and will have to resurrect a common awareness of the masculine and feminine archetypes. They will need to look into the past (beyond decades or centuries of heinous human cruelty and what is certain to be ghastly exploitation of women) in order to structure a new culture in which archetype, shadow, and gender are recognized—and reconciled.

Originally, *patriarchy* simply meant "rule by the fathers," but in modern times it has become synonymous with a system of power imposed by adult men. In ancient Africa, Egypt, and Mesopotamia, religion was structured around myriad female deities, and many of those societies were matriarchal, meaning that, for the most part, women held power and property rights.

The so-called pagan religions of the pre-Christian era were earth-based and female-honoring sects in which women ruled or power was shared equitably by women and men. Gnosticism, an early Christian sect, had its roots in the pagan mystery cults of Ancient Egypt and Greece and gradually began incorporating the Jesus myth. A brilliant trilogy by researchers Timothy Freke and Peter Gandy, *The Jesus Mysteries*, *Jesus and the Lost Goddess*, and *The Laughing Jesus*, explores the history of Gnosticism and its role in the early Christian church, as well as the ultimate rejection of the sect by the church fathers. Elaine Pagels, in her book *The Gnostic Gospels*, further illumines the drama between Gnosticism and the ecclesiastical hierarchy. Significant among the plethora of objections to Gnosticism by early church theologians was Gnosticism's insistence on the equal status of men and women.

Clerics such as Irenaeus and Eusebius—and especially Augustine—vehemently opposed Gnosticism. Among their specific objections are Gnosticism's polytheistic roots; its earth-based, mythological orientation; its commitment to the equal status of women; its resistance to the concept of original sin; and its reluctance to proclaim Jesus as God in human form. Struggles between the church hierarchy and a variety of Christian sects continued throughout antiquity, but by the end of the Second Council of Nicaea in 787, orthodoxy had triumphed, and peripheral Christian sects had fallen away.

The writings of church fathers reveal an irrational dread of the feminine archetype in general and women in particular. Augustine wrote,

"What is the difference whether it is in a wife or a mother, it is still Eve the temptress that we must beware of in any woman. . . . I fail to see what use woman can be to man, if one excludes the function of bearing children." And even more stunningly, "Women should not be enlightened or educated in any way. They should, in fact, be segregated as they are the cause of hideous and involuntary erections in men."

Much has been written on the patristic or patriarchal spirituality of the Roman Catholic Church by Catholic theologian Rosemary Radford Ruether, who describes herself as an ecofeminist. In her book *Gaia and God,* she offers an ecofeminist theology that presents a path toward earth healing and a template for integrated relationships between men and women, communities and nations. Ruether—along with other scholars exploring the aversion of early church fathers to the feminine archetype and earth-based spirituality—notes an unconscious or perhaps semiconscious association of nature with the feminine in the minds of many male clergy of antiquity. The notion of Mother Earth is deeply embedded in the human psyche, and early church theologians were no exception.

In his groundbreaking 1993 article "The Split between Spirit and Nature in European Consciousness," Ralph Metzner traces the church's shift, over the centuries, from a concern with earth stewardship to a desire for complete mastery of nature. He argues that this constitutes a split in the Western psyche between nature and spirituality in which "we feel we have to overcome our 'lower' animal instincts and passions, to conquer the body, in order to be spiritual and attain to 'heaven,' or 'enlightenment.' In the modern psychological, Freudian version, the conflict is between the human ego consciousness, which has to struggle against the unconscious body-based, animal id, in order to attain consciousness and truly human culture."

Deeply influenced by the social justice paradigm of Dorothy Day, an American Catholic activist in the 1930s, and Daniel and Philip Berrigan, activist priests in the 1960s, as well as by the writings of Rosemary Ruether, many Catholic nuns in the United States in the past fifty years have become increasingly liberal, both theologically and politically. While they have not openly supported abortion or contraception, they have struggled tirelessly to promote women's education and equality and have worked assiduously for human rights, civil rights, and the alleviation of poverty, to name only a few of their social justice causes.

In early 2012, the Vatican launched a new campaign to reign in "unruly" nuns in the United States. A Reuters/Huffington Post article entitled, "Vatican Crackdown on Nuns over Social Justice Issues, Women Ordination," reported that, according to the Vatican, "the nuns promoted political views at odds with those expressed by U.S. Roman Catholic bishops, 'who are the church's authentic teachers of faith and morals.' The Vatican chastised the nuns for airing discussions about the ordination of women, the church patriarchy and ministry to gay people." Not coincidentally, this crackdown neatly parallels the escalating "war on women" by the Republican Party in the United States, in which funding for contraception and abortion has been savagely cut, along with funding for programs that alleviate poverty.

Some observers speculate that the Vatican was particularly inflamed by Sister Margaret Farley's 2006 book, *Just Love: A Framework for Christian Sexual Ethics*. According to the Vatican, the book contradicted church teaching on issues like masturbation, homosexuality, and marriage and its author had a "defective understanding" of Catholic theology.

In a June 2012 interview by Paul Raushenbush, "In Praise of Courageous Nuns Facing the Vatican Crackdown," Sister Joan Chittister, described the Vatican's most recent campaign to reign in the nuns, "Well it is a hostile take over, there's no doubt about that. They're 'cleaning up the church'—everything but themselves." "Everything but themselves," of course, refers to the epidemic of sexual abuse among male priests worldwide.

Anyone familiar with the culture of these radical women religious knows that they are keenly aware of the plight of our planet, and many are consciously aware of and talking about the collapse of industrial civilization. More importantly, they are committed to living sustainably and self-sufficiently in community.

As noted by collapse author Dmitry Orlov in his 2012 article "Sustainable Living as Religious Observance," throughout history, many religious and monastic communities have developed interpersonal and logistical skills that superbly prepared them for navigating the collapse of societies around them. I believe that collapse-aware, activist nuns throughout the world are no exception to this pattern.

Societies in collapse typically become more reactionary, rigid, and ideological as they haltingly attempt to ward off total unraveling. In the United States, where the wheels are coming off more blatantly with every passing day, it is not surprising that politics is in gridlock and that the ruling elite in Congress is moving dramatically to the right. Simultaneously, the current administration moves the nation toward a total surveillance state, surpassing the former administration in scrutinizing its citizenry.

While the Obama administration affirms same-gender marriage, the war on women persists and will most certainly worsen in the coming years, regardless of which political party is in power. As collapse exacerbates, we can expect to see intensified scapegoating of immigrants, Muslims, and women. As cities implode economically, police forces, firefighters, and courts will vanish. As happened with the collapse of the Soviet Union, people will band together to protect themselves and each other, or they will not survive. How far down the scale of barbarity humans descend is anyone's guess.

But none of this is news. What fascinates me is not so much humanity's engulfment in darkness, but what kind of culture we will construct from the rubble of this one. For me, one thing is certain. If the authentic principles of the feminine and masculine archetypes do not inform our relationships with each other and with the earth community in the development of the next culture, we will have succeeded only in creating Civilization 2.0. I will not attempt to predict when humanity might reclaim its wholeness, fully confront its masculine and feminine shadow, and consciously live the more noble attributes of both archetypes, nor can I speculate how much suffering may be required for this to occur. I am certain, however, that the memory of gender equity from the twentieth and twenty-first centuries and from ancient times will not be entirely expunged. Archetypes may be ignored, but they are innate and instinctual and therefore cannot be eradicated.

The time to begin focusing on the revitalization of gender justice and wholeness is not after centuries of what is likely to be domination by the shadow, but here and now, by examining and working to heal the shadow masculine and feminine within ourselves and throughout the culture. Like the incorrigible, non-shirking nuns, we must begin wherever we are and confront patriarchy whenever it attempts to "rein us in" and carry out its hostile takeovers. In so doing, we facilitate the preservation of memory regarding the advances of oppressed groups in our lifetimes, even as the collapse of industrial civilization develops a life of its own.

The Elephant in Every Collapsing Room

Everyone preparing for collapse, by definition, wants to survive it. We are innately wired for survival, but unless we include the possibility of death in our preparation, we aren't really preparing. It's so easy to disregard death, especially if one is an American. As Ehrenreich noted above, our corporate, capitalist, happy-faced culture marinates us in positive thinking.

Last year, I stumbled onto an exposé of positive thinking by Mark Vernon, "The Secret: New Agey Mind Cure Still Pretending that 'Positive Thinking' Can Solve Everything." The addiction to a positive attitude in the face of the end of the world as we have known it is beyond irrational. It's an obsession that could only be cherished by humans; it is, indeed, human-centric—as if human beings are the only species that matter and as if the most crucial issue is that those humans are able to feel good about themselves as the world burns.

Usually, having a "positive" attitude about collapse implies wanting it not to happen and doing everything in one's power to convince oneself that it won't happen. This is a uniquely human attitude. If we could interview a polar bear that had just drowned trying to find food, because the ice shelves that it usually rested on during the hunt were no longer there, I suspect it would express a very different attitude. Of course, we have the delusional human element who argue that humans are not killing the planet—as if the hairy-eared dwarf lemur, the pygmy elephant, or the ruby topaz hummingbird were responsible. Who else has skyrocketed ocean acidity to exponential levels? Who else is inundating the atmosphere with carcinogens; turning topsoil into sand that contains as many nutrients as a kitchen sponge; and rapidly eliminating clean, drinkable water from the face of the earth?

Derrick Jensen, in *Endgame*, states, "The needs of the natural world are more important than the needs of any economic system." He continues, "Any economic system that does not benefit the natural communities on which it is based is unsustainable, immoral, and really stupid" (Seven Stories Press, 2006, 1.127–28).

Explaining the human disconnection from the rest of earth's inhabitants, Jensen describes the various layers of resistance among humans to their innate animal essence. One of the deeper layers is our "fear and loathing of the body"—that is, our instinctual wildness—and, therefore, our vulnerability to death, which causes us to distance ourselves from the reality that we, indeed, are animals.

Have not all modern societies disowned and committed genocide against the indigenous? And for what purpose? Not only for the purpose of stealing their land, eradicating their culture, and eliminating so-called barriers to "progress," but because native peoples (you know, "savages"), as a result of their intimate connection with nature, are such glaring reminders of humankind's animal nature. They are embarrassingly "uncivilized." Modernity must "civilize" the savage in order to excise the animal, inculcating in him a human-centric worldview. The consequence has been not only the incessant destruction of earth and its plethora of life forms but the murder of the human soul itself. Benjamin Franklin said it best, after returning from living with the Iroquois, "No European who has tasted Savage life can afterwards bear to live in our societies."

Any person who wants to maintain a "positive attitude" in this culture—the culture of civilization that is killing the planet, killing all the people and species that we all love—that person is irrational and deeply afflicted with denial. He is exactly like a member of an abusive family—a family in which physical and sexual assault are occurring on a daily basis—who insists on "thinking good thoughts" and resents anyone and everyone who speaks the truth about the abusive system.

So let's admit two things. (1) Humans are fundamentally animals. Yes, we are more than animals, but civilization, with its contempt for the feral, has inculcated us to own the "more than" and disown everything else. (2) The culture of civilization is inherently abusive, and it is abusive precisely because it has disowned the animal within the human. Indeed, animals kill other animals for survival, but they do not soil, conquer, rape, pillage, plunder, enslave, pollute, slash, burn, and poison their habitat—unlike those "more-than-animal" beings who seem incapable of *not* doing all of the above. Conversely, the "more-than-human" creatures respect their surroundings, because they instinctively sense that their survival depends on doing so.

Civilization, which has never ceased soiling its nest, has also never understood its proper place on the earth: a guest, a neighbor, a fellow member of the community of life. As a result, everything civilization has devised and which is "unsustainable, immoral, and stupid," as Jensen names it, is now in the process of collapsing.

Fundamentally, what all forms of positive thinking about collapse come down to is our own fear of death.

Thanks to civilization's Judeo-Christian tradition and its other hand-maiden, corporate capitalism, humans have become estranged from the reality that death is a part of life. Human hubris, gone berserk as a result of a tumescent ego, uncontained by natural intimacy with the more-than-human world, believes humanity to be omnipotent and entitled to invincibility. Therefore, from the human-centric perspective, "collapse should be stopped" or "maybe it won't happen" or "somehow humans will come to their senses." Meanwhile, the drowning polar bears inwardly wail for the death of humanity as the skeletons of formerly chlorophyll-resplendent Colorado spruce shiver and sob in the icy December wind. Our moral, spiritual, and human obligation is to discard our positive attitude and start feeling *their* pain. Until we do, we remain human-centric and incapable of seizing the multitudinous opportunities that collapse offers for rebirth and transformation of this planet and its human and more-than-human inhabitants.

May I remind us: we are *all* going to die. Or as Derrick Jensen writes in *Endgame*, "The truth is that I'm going to die someday, whether or not I stock up on pills. That's life. And if I die in the population reduction that takes place as a corrective to our having overshot carrying capacity, well, that's life, too. Finally, if my death comes as part of something that serves the larger community, that helps stabilize and enrich the landbase of which I'm part, so much the better"(123).

Now, I hasten to add that I am not suggesting we select our most "negative" emotion about collapse, move in, redecorate, and take up residence there. Feel one's feelings? Yes. And at the same time, revel in those aspects of one's life where one feels nourished, loved, supported, and comforted, and in those people and activities that give one joy and meaning. Had civilization not spent the last five thousand years attempting to murder the indigenous self, inherent in all humans, we would not have to be told—as native peoples and the more-than-human world do not—that, most of the time, life on this planet is challenging, painful, scary, sad, and sometimes enraging. What our indigenous ancestors had to sustain them through the dark times was ritual and community. Our work is to embrace and refine both, instead of intractably clinging to a "positive attitude" in the face of out-of-control, incalculable abuse and devastation.

Collapse and the Wild Self

> *To regard any animal as something lesser than we are, not equal to our own vitality and adaptation as a species, is to begin a deadly descent into the dark abyss of arrogance where cruelty is nurtured in the corners of certitude. Daily acts of destruction and brutality are committed because we fail to see the dignity of Other.*
>
> TERRY TEMPEST WILLIAMS

Every animal with whom I have developed a relationship in my adult life has been a teacher. Each has "spoken" to me in a different way, whether by lying beside me as I cried, warning me of impending danger, or just looking deeply into my eyes. Similarly, animals I have encountered in the wilds of nature have instructed me, comforted me, warned me, and enchanted me.

Countless studies in recent decades have revealed the uncanny intelligence and wisdom of the four-leggeds and others. Research with gorillas, chimpanzees, whales, dolphins, elephants, and many other species reveals their profound intelligence and intuition, as well as their emotion. It has been said that elephants never forget the smell of a tribesman and that they mourn their dead and engage in long-distance communication using barely audible, low-frequency growls. They have also been shown to be able to distinguish between different human tribes based on their smell and on color of their clothing.

It is axiomatic that in a collapsing world, some of the worst casualties of abuse and neglect will be members of the nonhuman world. Since the financial crisis of 2008, we have heard of innumerable abandoned animals left behind in the wake of massive housing foreclosures. We hear of jaw-dropping cases of hoarding and abuse. It seems that animals are the most expendable possession when disaster strikes, and animal shelters in times of disaster become inundated with unwanted or abandoned pets. We need only recall Katrina and other disasters, where pets are left behind or perish in heart-wrenching numbers, to imagine the toll that the collapse of civilization will take on the creatures.

Conversely, in many indigenous societies, animals are perceived as superb sentinels of danger. Humans in those cultures have learned to listen to the animals and watch their behavior for indications of shifts in weather patterns, impending disaster, and changes in the seasons. After the Indonesian tsunami of 2004, it was widely reported that many humans were entranced by countless glittering seashells that were exposed when the tides receded, and they were swept away by sudden walls of water, whereas herds of animals immediately ran to higher ground and survived. Tribal people respected the animals and followed their signals, but non-tribal people did not.

Therein lies a huge lesson for collapse-aware humans. In the great unraveling of civilization, animals may be our most useful companions, not only in alleviating our loneliness, but in enhancing our awareness.

The plight of animals, as collapse intensifies, will no doubt be heart-wrenching, but perhaps also dangerous. It will be impossible to keep all animals fed, and it will be impossible for hordes of surviving animals to find enough food to stay alive. Thus, we can expect many animals to become aggressive with each other and possibly with humans in an attempt to survive. Likewise, we can expect many starving humans to resort to hunting and eating all manner of animals that they previously would have never considered consuming. It will not be a pretty picture.

When I wrote about this topic in *Sacred Demise,* my focus was primarily on how we consume or do not consume animals in present time, particularly with respect to animals raised organically versus industrially. In this essay, I want to address specific issues around our relationships with animals in a collapsing world.

First, I want to emphasize the wildness of animals and the inescapable reality of our own "wild self" as human beings. As the world becomes more "uncivilized" (in the sense that the paradigm and rules of industrial civilization deteriorate and become more irrelevant), our species is likely to become more "uncivilized" on a variety of levels—some desirable and some undesirable. The dark side of this reality is that many people, terrified of what's happening and unable to make sense of it, will operate from the reptilian brain. This is not the kind of "wildness" to which I'm referring when I speak of the wild self. Rather, I'm talking about the fact that, because humans *are* animals, we can consciously use that reality to our advantage by deploying intuition and instinct to assist us in navigating a world unraveling. While maintaining our sense of dignity and commitment to doing no harm intentionally, we can draw on the wild self to assist us in being more instinctually resilient.

In order to experience the wild self, however, it is necessary to step back from the logical mind and be present in the body. Two wonderful resources for guiding us into inhabiting the body and the wild self are psychologist Bill Plotkin's books *Soulcraft* and *Nature and the Human Soul,* both of which I highly recommend. Plotkin has conducted vision quests and wilderness excursions with folks for decades and offers a treasure trove of wisdom regarding experiencing and utilizing our wild nature.

I suspect that in a collapsing world, this may be easier than we imagine. It is likely that we will be spending a great deal of time outdoors, and it is very unlikely that we will have ready access to a daily hot shower, soap, shampoo, toothpaste, or clean clothes. I recall an offhand comment by Dmitry Orlov in one of his presentations about how well one could live in terms of barter items during collapse if one had a shipping container of personal hygiene items. In summary, conditions are likely to be more conducive to accessing the animal self in a chaotic world.

This, of course, does not mean that we lose or sacrifice our humanity.

In fact, I believe that the collapse of industrial civilization will necessitate both living from our wildness *and* discovering how precious our humanity and the humanity of others really is.

Another aspect of our relationship with animals during collapse is our ability to care for them. While many of us who love our animals have probably amassed great quantities of pet food in preparation for collapse, at some point, it will run out. For our carnivore pets, it may or may not be easy to find sufficient animal flesh to feed them. Moreover, there is likely to be little, if any, veterinary care. If human health care is radically rationed or nonexistent, we can only imagine what kind of care will be available for animals. Therefore, I raise a very practical question, are you prepared to put your suffering animal (or a stray) out of its misery if it is starving or severely ill? Seasoned hunters may have no problem with this, but many others will. Likewise, we can expect that our pets will become prey for other starving animals—and people—so to what extent are we prepared to protect them?

I have never met anyone who is actively preparing for collapse who is not fond of animals. Perhaps that is because those individuals have allowed the non-humans to teach them about vulnerability, loyalty, sacrifice, risk, danger, loss, affection, and much more. Perhaps it is because something in us knows that over 150 non-human species go extinct each day, and we are yet another species, unable to predict when the collapse of civilization will manifest *our* extinction.

Because negativity is unknown to them, the creatures are superb teachers, writes Eckhart Tolle:

> No other life form on the planet knows negativity, only humans, just as no other life form violates and poisons the earth that sustains it. Have you ever seen an unhappy flower or a stressed oak tree? Have you ever come across a depressed dolphin, a frog that has a problem with self-esteem, a cat that cannot relax, or a bird that carries hatred and resentment? The only animals that may occasionally experience something akin to negativity or show signs of neurotic behavior are those that live in close contact with humans

and so link into the human mind and its insanity. Watch any plant or animal and let it teach you acceptance of what is, surrender to the Now. I have lived with several Zen masters—all of them cats (*The Power of Now: A Guide to Spiritual Enlightenment,* 190).

We will become more teachable and develop more capacity to learn from the creatures as we ourselves become more "creaturely." Civilization has disowned wildness as primitive and inimical to "progress." It has inculcated shame in us regarding our bodily functions, fluids, odors, and needs. Driven by religion and the Puritan ethic, our sexuality is often estranged from our innately animal instincts. To be "civilized" is synonymous with being domesticated, restrained, and repressed, and if we participate in sexual behavior at all, we are encouraged to do so in a controlled, sanitized, or even surreptitious fashion.

Obviously, functional human beings interacting with other human beings must adhere to limits and boundaries. Paradoxically, however, the more we celebrate our inherent animal nature, the more likely we are to effortlessly honor our limits. We have only to notice that it is not animals that are soiling their nests and desecrating their habitat, but humans.

A post-petroleum world is likely to be one where mobility will be strictly limited to walking, horseback riding, or riding in animal-drawn carts with wooden wheels. Large-scale farming will not be possible unless draft animals are used. Consequently, humans will become dependent on animals for transportation and energy, as we were in earlier times, and this will undoubtedly transform our relationships with them.

Collapse will offer more opportunities than we might imagine for connectedness with other species. From house pets to draft animals, to those we must kill and eat, to those that will tell us what time of day or what time of life it is, the creatures must and will be our companions. They have lessons to teach us. Can we listen and learn?

Civilization has given us "dominion" over the earth and its creatures, but in the new paradigm, the creatures will be the elders, the truly wise ones who have come to help us remember our animal origins and our animal destiny.

Collapsing Interdependently

In the United States, nearly one-fifth of all people do not have enough food to eat. Children need foster care; aging seniors need eldercare. In each instance, few services are available to provide the most vulnerable of our society with what they need. Almost none of the services from the old days of "social programs" are still in place, and we are quickly approaching a time when the streets of the United States may begin to resemble those of Calcutta.

Most of my readers are not survivalists. Most are not coming from the perspective of "my family, my homestead, my needs first." Yet I'm quite certain that from time to time, we all ponder the reality of millions of people around us who do not have food or water, and we wonder what our world will be like when thousands of children and the elderly are abandoned in the streets because their families cannot care for them—and what decisions we might have to make when confronted with these situations. Even if we have given this a great deal of thought, it is important to understand that this issue is not one that can be resolved intellectually. We cannot decide with certainty how we might handle such situations in advance. While we might mentally adopt a "policy" toward the needy, so many situations will be circumstantial, and what will be most valuable will not necessarily be a sharp intellect but a well-honed intuition.

I believe that one thing that could greatly assist us in the future is current-time involvement with alleviating suffering in our immediate environment. Yes, I know, there is so much of it that one can easily become overwhelmed, but if the amount of suffering is enormous now, consider how large it will be in the future. You may already have contact with the most vulnerable in our world, and you may be doing your best to support them, but if you aren't, there are a number of ways to make this happen.

It is important to know our neighbors, not only for security purposes, but to know what they might need from us that they may be too proud to reveal. Are you sure that you neighbors have enough to eat? If not, you can engage them in conversations about food prices—a topic about which almost everyone has something to say these days.

We live in a culture that fosters dependence. Even if we grow up, go to college, and pursue the American dream, we are, in a sense, following a path of dependence—dependence on a myth, a fantasy that says that if you work hard, pay your bills, and play by the rules, you will succeed. It all *looks* very self-sufficient, but ultimately, following the myth is about relying on the government and the nation's institutions to also play by the rules and be there when you need them. Now that the American dream is dead and buried, millions of Americans are lost, emotionally ravaged, or are turning to addictions or suicide, because they simply cannot cope with the death of the dream. Many still depend on a grocery store for their food, and many continue to hope that some president or legislator will save them from the inevitable.

On the other hand, many of us, including some who are collapse-aware, have "declared their independence" from the system. Perhaps we bought out of it years ago and pride ourselves in self-sufficiency. Those of the survivalist persuasion are preparing their "doomsteads" and bug-out plans for an isolated existence far from highly populated areas—and woe to those who would trespass on their fortress. Independence is more functional than dependence, but it has its limits. No one can store enough food to last for the rest of his or her life. Eventually, independence must be transcended.

The interdependent individual recognizes that she or he cannot survive without the assistance and cooperation of others. When one's cache of food and supplies runs out, one will need to have networks of cooperation in place. Practicing interdependence in current time is crucial preparation for full-blown collapse and a world of very limited resources. For some, especially for those who feel safer being independent, interdependence is challenging, perhaps even emotionally threatening. All the more reason for cultivating it sooner rather than later.

Volunteering in a homeless shelter, a daycare center for homeless children, a nursing home, or other agencies still in existence that serve vulnerable populations is excellent psychological preparation for a time when none of these services exists. First, it puts you in a serving mode. You allow your innate compassion to reach out to other human beings in need. In addition, it causes you to ponder how you might deal with situations in the future when members of the population you are serving are symbolically or literally on your doorstep. Furthermore, it expands your horizons beyond "me and mine" to a sense of the commons and a camaraderie with the rest of humanity.

During the Great Depression, my grandfather worked for the U.S. Postal Service—one of the few secure jobs of that era. He also lived near a railroad around which moved a great number of hoboes and men who were hopping freight trains, bound for other parts of the country in search of employment. On a telephone pole in front of his house, he posted a sign that read, "Hungry? Knock on the door." In all his years of offering food to travelers, no one ever abused my grandfather's invitation, and my grandparents served many meals to weary but well-behaved travelers.

Now I realize that collapse will not unfold in the same way as did the Great Depression, but sharing food for barter—or for nothing in exchange—may establish relationships that later result in added security and even community building.

There is something about being of service in current time that could have lasting benefits for us in the future, simply because a service mentality and especially a willingness to see the suffering of others in this moment provide us with critical emotional skills. In many cases, we may need to provide nothing except the capacity to listen.

Two decades ago, when I lived in Northern California, the Russian River flooded the town of Guerneville and drove thousands of people in western Sonoma County out of their homes. The Sonoma County Human Services Department opened up a shelter for many flood refugees in the Santa Rosa Veterans Building and sent out a number of public service announcements asking for volunteers to come to the Vets Building and sit with the people who had been traumatized by the flood. I was among the volunteers and spent several evenings sitting with people who were living temporarily in the shelter. What I noticed in every case was that they simply needed someone to listen to their story. They had food and shelter, but they needed to tell someone what happened to them and just be heard.

One of the most important skills we can develop for collapse is the capacity to listen. We may encounter people who have been walking or living alone for days or weeks and haven't had anyone to speak with—or even if they had company, they may not have felt safe talking with them. Moreover, we may find *ourselves* in a situation where we have become isolated and just want someone to listen to us.

On the one hand, it is imperative that we take care of ourselves and our loved ones, but at the same time, it is crucial to serve other human beings. As I've already stated, we may be forced to make difficult, even wrenching, decisions about whom to assist, how to assist, and when, and we must be very attuned to our intuition in order to do so.

One of myriad reasons that industrial civilization is collapsing is its fundamental focus on the individual. "It's all about me, screw the commons," is the essential mantra of modernity—it is independence on steroids. Because this attitude is inimical to our humanity, it is not sustainable, and, in fact, it is destroying our species and our planet. I venture to say that most collapse-aware individuals cherish some fantasies, no matter how frail or infrequently spoken of, of a new culture in which we live in authentic community, sharing resources, food, tasks, and recreation with each other. And we already know that such a culture will not be possible without an attitude of service and cooperation.

It's easier to establish interdependent relationships over time with neighbors or acquaintances and harder to forge such connections in the moment and with strangers. A background in service can assist with the latter, particularly if we value the red flags our intuition might be sending us, as well as the green lights that tell us that it's okay to help.

I believe that it is one thing to work on building interdependence in Transition groups or Common Security Clubs in current time, when life is much less challenging than it will be in the future. But a rapidly unfolding, full-blown collapse will test our ability to serve and to cooperate, and only then will we discover the extent to which we are capable of these. Furthermore, it is much easier to build cooperative relationships with individuals who are fundamentally like us than it is to build them with those who, for a variety of reasons, may be very different.

If you are not currently engaged in service of some kind, I invite you to open yourself to that possibility and sit with what kind of service and to whom you might feel drawn. How can you utilize the service to which you feel drawn or in which you are engaged to prepare yourself for a deepening collapse? What skills do you have to offer? What skills could a service project further develop in you?

This is not about bleeding-heart caretaking of everyone and everything around us. Boundaries must be established and limits set; very, very tough choices will have to be made. However, developing an attitude of *inter*-dependence with our fellow earthlings and actually seeking ways to serve them engenders ever-new attitudes and skills that may improve the quality of our lives—or even save our lives—during very daunting times.

What Myth Will Replace the American Dream?

There is a thinking in primordial images, in symbols which are older than the historical man, which are inborn in him from the earliest times, eternally living, outlasting all generations, still make up the groundwork of the human psyche. It is only possible to live the fullest life when we are in harmony with these symbols; wisdom is a return to them.

CARL JUNG

Unfortunately, American modernity, with its short memory and determination to distance itself from all things ancient, has misapprehended the importance of myth, all the while living out what was a sacrosanct myth called the American dream. Twenty-first century humans generally define *myth* as something that is not true and use the word synonymously with *fantasy* or *delusion*. At its root, however, *myth* is related to *mystery, story,* and *word*. The ancient writers and speakers of myth did not consider myths to be falsehoods but a series of lies or tall tales that speak the truth. That is to say, myths are inherently paradoxical but intended to convey profound lessons.

Barry Spector, author of *Madness at the Gates of the City: The Myth of American Innocence,* defines *myth* as "the stories we tell ourselves about ourselves. They organize and justify experience and speak to our unresolved conflicts, needs, and fantasies. . . . We turn to myth to comprehend the elemental forces that move through our lives, to know who we are, to understand which stories inform our consciousness"(19). In other words, we use myths to make sense of our lives or, in many instances, to justify or defend them. The American dream is a myth we evolved to explain both our history and our exceptionalism.

We assume that, in the modern world, ancient stories such as Greek myths have no relevance to our lives, yet all myths and stories are replete with archetypal themes. Archetypes are merely motifs in the human psyche that, under certain circumstances and in the midst of specific experiences, become activated or constellated and can influence our current reality. For example, the *mother* archetype is present in the psyche of every woman, but it becomes highly activated when a woman is carrying a child and preparing to give birth, and it remains activated throughout her life as she fulfills the role of mothering. Even if a woman never has a child, her maternal energy is likely to appear at some point in her life, and when it does, the mother archetype is stirred and will inform how she manages her caretaking.

When we consider the myth of the American dream, for example, a number of archetypes become obvious. Before exploring this notion, let's look at the essential contents of the American dream. It goes something like this.

The United States is the land of opportunity. Our ancestors came here fleeing persecution in Europe and, in doing so, discovered that if they worked hard and were willing to make sacrifices, they could not only live freely but could become successful at anything they undertook. Over the centuries, their hard work produced a society in which people could begin at the very bottom of the economic ladder and rise to the top. Eventually—and particularly after World War II—they created a middle-class existence in which they could acquire gainful employment and, on the basis of their hard work, receive promotions and all manner of rewards. They could buy a home at a reasonable price, have full health insurance for themselves and their families, build a generous retirement package, put their kids through college, and spend their golden years traveling or pursuing hobbies that they had no time to pursue when they were working hard, carving out their American dream. At the end of life, they will have paid for their funerals in advance and will leave a generous inheritance for their descendants.

So let's notice the archetypal themes in the myth: land of opportunity, ancestors, persecution, triumph over adversity, success, heroism, entitlement, elderhood, prosperity, legacy.

Exploring each in depth would be a fascinating study, but more importantly, let's also notice what is *not* part of the story: the conquest and genocide of millions of indigenous people that made this kind of astonishing success possible; the privileges afforded to people of Anglo ethnicity; the role of war and resource exploitation in creating a flourishing economy; the basic assumption that health care is a human right; the assumption that young people should have access to a fundamental college education; and the assumption that at a certain age, the biology of most humans begins to slow down, and they need to work less and enjoy their leisure time more.

Some of these themes are incredibly dark, and others are assumptions that the middle class adopted in order to achieve a desirable quality of life. Nevertheless, what stories omit is equally as important as what they disclose. The American dream is a mixed story: in part, a story of genocide, racism, classicism, geopolitical and resource imperialism, exceptionalism, and entitlement—as well as a set of humanitarian assumptions about what constitutes a rich quality of life.

Nearly all myths contain mixed themes and feature complicated characters who possess qualities that are both "good" and "bad."

Perhaps the most important reality excluded from the American dream is the fate of all heroes. The hero (or heroine) is an archetype. The hero sets out to complete a task that the gods (or an inner voice) have ordered. His or her efforts soon become a journey of struggle with forces opposed to the task. If the hero becomes a victim of hubris, that is, a prisoner of his or her own ego, forgetting the original mission that was ordered by some greater power, the hero will fail, sometimes suddenly, sometimes gradually.

The hero may return home, having learned a number of spiritual or philosophical lessons, or the hero may become entangled by his or her own foibles and learn nothing—or may even be consumed with hubris and thereby fall, literally or symbolically. A classic example of the latter would be the Greek myth of Icarus. Icarus and his father, Daedalus, tried to escape from Crete using wings that Daedalus had made of feathers and wax. Icarus forgot his father's instructions not to fly too high, the sun's heat melted the wax that held the feathers together, and Icarus fell into the sea and drowned.

Sooner or later, the heroic perspective must be tempered by "the gods" or, if you prefer, life. Once the hero chooses to humble himself or herself, he or she is no longer a "hero" and becomes quintessentially human. To be human is to acknowledge one's vulnerability and lack of invincibility and, most importantly, to grasp one's interdependence with forces beyond oneself. If heroic individuals (or cultures) refuse to be tempered, humbled, and instructed by life, they will ultimately and inevitably encounter their demise.

The American dream is nothing if not heroic, and it has never recognized what happens to all heroes who refuse to learn from the lessons of their journey. So whether you choose to perceive the dissolution of the American dream as the hero's journey or as the collapse of industrial civilization—or both—the American dream was fated to fail each time the collective refused to be instructed by something greater than itself.

The question now at hand is, what myth might replace the American dream? The question assumes, however, that America as we know it will (or should) endure physically as a contiguous stretch of land between two oceans, and it also assumes that as America's demise accelerates, the dominant culture will prevail alongside a number of subcultures. What I suspect are more accurate assumptions are that (1) the geography of the continental United States may, at some point, be fragmented severely or perhaps unrecognizably by a variety of geological changes; (2) a rotting infrastructure will eventually result in dramatic estrangement of regions from one another; (3) new myths will be constructed by local populations, who will form their own autonomous cultures. Old stories will be retold and parsed for those aspects that might be useful to retain and utilize and those aspects that might be eliminated entirely.

I might have chosen any number of stories to insert here, but this one keeps nagging me. It comes from West Africa's tribal tradition and conveys some arresting symbolism that is deeply relevant to our time.

One day, a young man and young woman were walking through a field of flowers. It was a lovely summer day. Birds were singing; the sun was sparkling between the leaves of lush, green trees; the air was soft and fragrant with the flowers; and the sky was cloudless. Suddenly, the young man and woman saw ahead of them, off in the distance, a man who appeared to be waving at them. They kept walking toward him, and soon enough, they realized the man was waving at them to come closer, and they also realized that he was their father. Now this greatly surprised them, since a few weeks prior, their father had died.

As they came close to their father, he said, "Come with me. I have something I want you to see." They followed him as he walked into the field and then began walking into an opening in the ground. He descended into the earth, and they followed behind him on a small path, and then the path expanded into a regular road. Finally, they came to what looked like a village, but no people were around.

Then their father stopped and said to them, "Go over there and hide behind those bushes and watch. Watch very carefully. I'm going to go away, but I will return, and when I do, I want you to tell me what you saw."

The boy and girl waited patiently, and finally many people from the village came and stood in the center of it. They just stood there for a while, and then, soon enough, a man who had the appearance of a chief came toward the people. They made way for him, and he came and stood in the center of them. Then the chief turned, and the boy and girl noticed that one side of his body was covered with rotting flesh and was infested with maggots.

As soon as he showed this to the villagers, they approached him and began pulling off the rotting flesh and removing the maggots. After a while, that side of his body was clean and the flesh there was healthy.

Then the chief walked away into the darkness. Soon after, the people left as well. As their father had told them to do, the boy and girl just waited there behind the bush. Then, after a while, the people from the village came back into the center and just stood there. And, soon enough, the man who looked like the chief came back. This time, he revealed that one side of his body was covered with gold, and the people approached him and began polishing the gold on that side of his body until it was as shiny as the sun the boy and girl had just seen as they were walking in the flower-filled field. After a while, the people stopped polishing the gold, and the chief again left and walked away into the darkness. The people also went away, and the boy and girl remained behind the bush.

It wasn't long until their father came again and asked them what they had seen. They recounted to him the coming of the people and then the chief; the maggots, the rotting flesh, and how the people had removed them; and then how the chief and the people went away. The boy and girl also told him how the people came back and the chief came back and how he showed them the golden side of his body and how the people polished it. They told him how the chief and the people went away, and how they remained behind the bush until their father returned.

Then their father motioned to them to follow him. They did so and continued back on the road on which they had come, until they again found the narrow path and the opening into the upper world. They were back again in the beautiful field with the sun, the birds, the flowers, and the trees. Their father just stood there, and they walked past him across the field. They began to talk about what they had seen in the underworld and how it is that there is an upper world and an underworld and how it is that there is light and dark in the world—maggots and rotting flesh at one time and brilliant gold at another time.

The story ends as we leave the young man and woman walking through the field having this discussion.

Let's notice the archetype of the elder and the young man and woman—the opposites of youth and elder in the story. Very important is the fact that the father wanted to teach his children a lesson, but could not do so when he was alive and definitely could not do so in the upper world, in the light of day. Their willingness to follow death and descend to the underworld was essential.

What they witnessed was a series of crucial events. They witnessed a phenomenal event of community acceptance and support. The people did not judge the chief when one side of his body was covered with maggots and rotting flesh. Rather, they joined together to help heal him. When the community understands that we are all wounded and need each other in order to heal, deep healing can occur—in everyone.

Nor did they judge him when the other side of his body was covered with gold. There was no envy or jealousy that one side of his body was golden. Instead, they simply polished the gold to make it brighter and more brilliant. The gold might symbolize each person's gifts, what we have to offer the world. In the same way that the caring community helps heal its members, the community also polishes and supports everyone's talents and skills, without jealousy or competition.

Each time I hear or read or tell this story, I am struck with these merciful and caring acts of the community. Yes, the man they tended to was similar to a chief or perhaps *was* their chief, but the story does not convey a sense of subservience. Rather, one feels as if this is what the people are accustomed to doing—with each other, regardless of status in the community. Authority figure or not, the fact is that one side of his body was covered with maggots and rotting flesh. He was sick and needed healing.

Also in the story there is the ascent into the upper world by the father and the children. With every descent to the dark places, there is an ascent once again to beauty and lightness. We just never get to know exactly when that might happen. As I say when I tell stories, it happens "after a long time or a short time or whatever time it is."

Perhaps the most important detail of the story comes when the young man and young woman "walk past their father" in the upper world. This is a story of an elder reaching out to teach the young person a lesson that can only be experienced in the underworld. As a result, the wise and transformed young person comes back from the ordeal and "walks past" the elder. Whatever lessons the elder might impart, the wise younger person will—and should—"walk past them" in terms of becoming even wiser. The boy and girl are forever changed, they do not walk through the beautiful field mindlessly discussing the weather or boyfriends or girlfriends, but how it is that there is light and dark in the world, maggots and rotting flesh on one side of a person and bright, shining gold on the other side.

Some of the themes that come to mind as I tell the story are simplicity, death, life, beauty, upper world, underworld, the intimate connection of youth and elder, the healing and polishing power of the community.

I invite you to think about the part or parts of the story that most captured your attention. Whatever that part is, it has something important for you to reflect on.

There is no one story that will replace the American dream, but stories like this one—and there are thousands—can inform the myth or myths we create for building and preserving the next culture. In order to do so, however, we must recognize that we cannot live without myth, for it is an essential part of our humanity. If we attempt to do so—given the fact that something in us needs myth—we will only create more myths that echo the American dream—with themes of heroism, greed, entitlement, narcissism, exploitation, exceptionalism, and myriad abuses of power. How we prepare for and navigate collapse will provide the raw materials for the myths we make and will live by in a postindustrial world.

The Deeper Meaning
of Debt

*We need to invent a money system aligned with the new story that will
replace it.*

CHARLES EISENSTEIN

At this writing, the United States, along with a number of European
countries, is teetering on the edge of default. Even if a compromise
solution is reached by the two political parties, this will only be a band-aid
for the inevitable: total global economic meltdown.

How is it that in the past ten to twenty years, so many nations, families, and individuals have accumulated ghastly amounts of debt? We all
know individuals who live beyond their means, but how have entire cultures and countries lived so far beyond their means that repayment is not
even possible? How did this happen, and what are the assumptions and
attitudes that created a global debt/default nightmare?

In order to begin making sense of this, we need to address the very
basic definition of *debt*. Many collapse-aware individuals believe that the
fundamental problem with debt is usury, or charging interest. Yet, while
usury has been the culprit throughout history in the myriad catastrophes
around debt, it is not the root of the problem, and pointing to usury as
such does not go far enough in understanding the archetype or universal
theme of debt in the human psyche.

Debt means owing something to another person. It may be money, or it may be time, energy, effort, or responsibility. Debt means borrowing something from someone with a promise to pay it back. The moment two parties agree on a debt arrangement, there is a differentiation of power. The status of the lender has changed from equal to superior, and the status of the borrower has changed from equal to inferior. Thus, debt is a power relationship as much as an economic one. The most important word here is *relationship*, and debt changes the nature of the relationship between individuals.

I would argue that *debt itself* is a fundamental problem. For the borrower, a relationship of dependence is established. The lender has something that I need, and I am indebted to her. For the lender, the borrower is now dependent on my lending to him what he needs, and he is indebted to me.

Sometimes borrowing/lending can be a relationship of interdependence, when both parties are clear about their intentions and responsibly fulfill their obligations. In the current global debt meltdown, however, interdependence is not part of the equation. Rather, in the modern world, debt has become a power relationship exploited by both parties involved. For example, when a developing nation borrows money from the International Monetary Fund, in addition to interest, that nation is saddled with agreements regarding its development, which invariably require it to open its doors to a plethora of corporate influences that exploit its resources and people. Consequently, in this case, debt equals rape.

When the United States borrows money from other countries, it becomes temporarily beholden economically to the lending country but often agrees to provide the lender with massive amounts of weaponry in return for monetary loans. In this case, debt equals bribery.

For the earliest humans, lending and borrowing evolved as a way for people to help each other, and it was taken very seriously. There were consequences in the community for not repaying debt. If your ox, a primary source of livelihood, gets trapped in a pool of quicksand, and the repayment of your debt to me is long overdue, I may not be too quick to help you extricate your ox. However, if you have repaid me or are repaying me, I may be very glad to help you. Okay, so much for hunter-gatherer FICO scores.

Debt is not just some matter-of-fact business transaction. It is loaded with emotional and ethical issues that are more easily managed in small communities or between individuals than by complex financial behemoths.

The fact that money is attached to ethical and emotional issues indicates that it is highly charged and that it signifies something in the human psyche far greater and more significant than mere exchange. That "something" in the psyche is none other than the concept of *value*. Value means what something is worth, and it also means what is important to us—the principles by which we live that are based on notions of fairness, reciprocity, and empathy. It is impossible to extricate money from value; we can't engage in financial transactions exclusively from the intellect. Implicit in all transactions is value or values.

I do not wish to idealize our ancient ancestors or imply that their existence was an idyllic nest of the highest human values. In times as simple as theirs, however, value was perceived differently. They lived far more interdependently than we do because the survival of everyone depended on the welfare of each individual. They believed—and knew from direct experience—that if one person were in need, ultimately, everyone in the community would be in need. One of their fundamental values was the principle of give and take. I give to you when you need something, and you give to me when I need something.

I believe that deep in our species memory is the recollection of ancient times when the exchange of resources was based on *gift* and *need*. In other words, most humans gifted other humans with what they needed, knowing that, in time of need, they would be gifted with what they needed in return.

In his book, *Sacred Economics: Money, Gift, and Society in the Age of Transition*, Charles Eisenstein notes, "Money is a system of social agreements, meanings, and symbols that develops over time. It is, in a word, a story, existing in social reality along with such things as laws, nations, institutions, calendar and clock time, religion, and science. Stories bear tremendous creative power. . . . Stories give meaning and purpose to life and therefore motivate action. Money is a key element of the story of Separation that defines our civilization" (Evolver Editions, 2011, 2).

Hence, money is all about relationship and stories—the story of how we came to be, the story of who we have become. The ancient, indigenous story taught that every member of the earth community is sacred, that is to say, connected with something greater than the mind and the senses. Each is inestimably precious and valuable.

Whenever we desire to give a gift, receive a gift, or feel gratitude, we experience the sacred, which, as I have stated many times, has nothing to do with religion or dogma. Inherent in giving, receiving, and feeling grateful is relationship, as opposed to separation. Before money, people bartered, gave gifts, and took care of each other materially out of a sense of gratitude and community. And not infrequently, gift giving involves sacrifice. People choose to give something away that they value dearly and may never have again, but they do so because giving the gift feels so important and because they value the relationship they have with the receiver.

In *Sacred Economics,* Eisenstein defines and expounds on the *gift economy* to which he believes humanity will eventually return as the money system fails. To reiterate: the economics of the ancients was based on relationship, whereas the economy of modernity has been based on separation. The assumption of the former was that money is sacred and connected with something greater than the five physical senses—that is to say, resources are sacred. Our relationship with resources, from this perspective, is nothing less than a relationship with the sacred. Moreover, our use of resources is relational as well. We do not use them in a vacuum, but in connection with all other beings. Enter another value in the Sacred Economy: accountability.

The gift economy is based on two essential principles: (1) a new story of humanity and how humans interact with each other based on abundance rather than scarcity; and (2) relationship, as opposed to separation. Adopting a new story and making relationship central to human interaction provide the potential for Sacred Economics to unfold.

If, as you read this, you are muttering under your breath, "Bah, humbug! Humans will never live this way," I must agree with you, in part. Our species, in its present state, refuses to live this way, but I have little doubt that as a result of many years, perhaps even a century, of bloodshed, famine, thirst, psychosis, and the annihilation of ghastly numbers of humans, we will come to understand within the marrow of our bones that the old story, and the separation on which it is based, cannot work, and that we must return to the wisdom of our ancestors.

So what are you hearing here? A theme that I state repeatedly in my work: hold in your mind the reality of what is and what is yet to come and, at the same time, hold in your heart the vision of what is possible for a transformed humanity, no matter how few in numbers, that is willing to step over the evolutionary threshold and become a new kind of human being. Trust me, that is the most difficult work you will ever do, and none of us does it perfectly.

So here we are in the twenty-first century, on the edge of a global debt catastrophe. How did we get here, and what must be done?

Obviously, based on what I have written above, modern humans created a story diametrically opposed to the story on which the ancients based their societies. For modernity, separation is the *modus operandi* of humanity. Humans are separated from each other, from the earth, and from themselves. As Thomas Berry notes, when we "other-ize" the earth and our fellow humans, we easily move from giving to taking, because separation implies that there will never be enough and that one must conquer and claim what one acquires out of one's own efforts. Thus, we *have* a relationship with people and things, but it is a *use* relationship, rather than a relationship of giving and receiving.

In the United States, installment buying originated near the turn of the twentieth century, with the advent of the automobile. It was now possible to purchase a new car over time, as opposed to paying for it in one lump sum. This was not an easy sell at first, because so many Americans were not used to borrowing money and would do so only in dire emergencies. Through the 1920s and the Great Depression, most people were reluctant to borrow, but with the close of World War II, everything changed. We could say that this is when American society got its first taste of the "mind-altering substance" of consumption. An entire society went from deprivation to indulgence in just a few short years, and, of course, none of it would have been possible without cheap and abundant oil.

The generation that lived through the Depression and World War II told itself that it "deserved" the suburban lifestyle and all of the things that cheap oil and a postwar economy made possible. Entitlement burgeoned, and the boomers were born to parents who compensated for their former deprivation by giving them everything they could possibly want and more.

As growth became the religion of a society of consumption addicts, debt became a sacrament. In fact, status in the religion became measured by the amount of debt one could take on and still hold a high FICO score. In this religion, much was sacrificed, but unlike the sacrifices involved in giving, these sacrifices were all about taking—sacrificing children, the earth, human emotion, all manner of relationships, and, yes, one's own physical body.

And so it seemed that hordes of fully grown adults began to regress and become nothing less than infantile in relation to their debt. Entitlement reigned, and few were willing to let debt stand between them and everything they wanted. It became a culture of two-year-olds who were incapable of accepting limits—that dirty L-word, synonymous with deprivation, doing without, and living within one's means. Simplicity? What are you talking about? You've got to be kidding! Never again will we permit anything like the Great Depression! Never again will we permit ourselves to even approach the sensation of deprivation. Never again will we settle for less than having it all.

But, oh, how unsustainable it all was—and is! The joy ride in daddy's convertible is over—nothing left but a twisted mass of metal, glass, and human carnage—humanity's "cost of living." As John Seed asks, "How long will earth allow us not to pay for our sins against her?"

In the 1990s, when I was drowning in credit card debt, I declared bankruptcy, but not before attending a year of Debtors Anonymous meetings—perhaps the best investment of my time in relation to the debt delusion I had bought into. In those meetings, and with the support of other members, I learned to pay constant attention to my money, know at all times what was in my bank account, and live within my means. Today I see around me a global train wreck of debt created by adolescents who were hell bent on having the last binge, screaming, "I want! I want!" all the way to individual and national default. However, the bills are now coming due for humanity. Sadly, the most disadvantaged and deprived will pay the bills for those who refused to live within limits.

The way out is not around, over, under, or above, but *through* the consequences we have created. We are being forced to look at our "cost of living," a lifestyle based on separation and a very outdated story. As a result of our debt disease, we are being compelled to respect—which literally means, "to look again"—our life purpose. Or, as Charles Eisenstein writes, "To be fully alive is to accept the guidance of the question, 'What am I here for?' "(283).

In the new culture Eisenstein writes about in *Sacred Economics*—not a culture that erupts suddenly, but one into which we transition—there will be no money and probably no debt. The innumerable losses of industrial civilization's collapse will, over time, bring forth a new story and a new relationship with people, resources, things, and the earth. It will necessitate living as if our very breath is a gift and every person in our lives is an opportunity to pass on the gifts we have received. The death of the old paradigm and all of the trappings of industrial civilization will provide space to forge new values, new relationships, and minimize, if not completely obliterate, the concept of *debt* from human consciousness.

Hospice Workers for the World

In 2007 the film *What a Way to Go: Life at the End of Empire* was released by filmmakers Tim Bennett and Sally Erickson. In a subsequent blogpost, referring to those consciously preparing for collapse, Erickson spoke of becoming "hospice workers for the world." On the one hand, she was referring to literally attending the death of fellow earthlings in the collapse process, but, more generally, her reference extended symbolically to attending the death of empire, industrial civilization, and a way of life.

Like many authors and storytellers, I am intrigued with symbolism and the role it plays in the conscious and unconscious mind, and lately I have returned to contemplating what it means to be a hospice worker for the world. Clearly, this return has been inspired by accompanying a very close friend in his struggle with myelodysplastic syndrome (MDS), a preleukemia illness. As with any life-threatening illness, there is no guarantee of survival. Being in daily contact with my friend, I have found myself deeply involved in his precarious journey and at times feeling very much like a hospice worker.

This experience motivated me to revisit the notion of collapse-aware individuals as hospice workers for the world—and, I hasten to add, for ourselves. Thus the questions: How do I accompany other human beings in literal or symbolic death? How am I to be present with myself as a way of life, a cultural paradigm, and perhaps as my own body dies? How do I allow things to die that need to die? How do I open to another way of life and allow myriad death experiences, both literal and symbolic, to remake me?

Perhaps the place to begin is to notice what *hospice* means and what the role of the hospice worker is. The word *hospice* is derived from the Latin *hospes,* which means both "host" and "guest, visitor." It is related to *hospitality* and *hospitable.* The earliest uses of *hospice* pertained to providing a temporary home for weary travelers, then became associated with providing a home for the aged and terminally ill. In the 1970s, the first hospice movement was formed, largely as a result of the research into death and dying done by Dr. Elisabeth Kübler-Ross. It is important to understand, however, that hospice work does not always assume that the patient is terminally ill or that death is the only prognosis or outcome. Thus, hospice work may or may not be about accompanying people through the death experience; it is about being present with them in their illness, whatever the end result may be.

In the current moment, as we scan our environment, we see a global economic system in collapse, ecosystems ready to draw their last breaths, a worldwide nuclear power crisis, and the likelihood of protracted resource wars that may extend decades beyond current time. If we allow ourselves to recognize our feelings about this, it may seem as if we have become permanent residents in a terminal cancer ward. People, paradigms, and cherished ways of life are dying everywhere. Overwhelmingly, our fellow earthlings are in massive denial about this ubiquitous death. Consciously, they kick and scream and mutter platitudes about technology finding a way to save the planet, even as they know at the deepest level that the human species is killing everything in sight, including itself.

While it is tempting to shove death in their faces in order to force them to wake up—or to write them off completely—neither reaction is likely to be useful. One must simply continue living one's life, preparing for the future, and if and when individuals around us seek our assistance, we can clarify that they and their species are facing a terminal illness. We can help them "die" to a way of life to which they have become addicted—or, in an actual emergency situation, perhaps we will be confronted with whether or not we are willing to assist them in dying literally.

Anyone who is speaking truth about collapse and supporting people in facing and preparing for it is, in a sense, a hospice worker for the world. And even when our friends or loved ones reject us, revile us, or remove themselves from us, we have a role in helping them "die" to industrial civilization—and the real truth is that they *know* that. Thus the myriad pushbacks we receive from them when we say what is so. After all, who wants to hear that their very identity—the industrially civilized ego they have built throughout their entire lives, the ego that defines who they are—is, well, dying?

But what about our own egos? How much have we allowed ourselves to "die" to the old paradigm? A lot, you say? Well, I invite you to think again. It's difficult to say with certainty how much of the ego has receded and how connected with a new paradigm we are until we are in crisis. Typically, the various crises of our current lives—job loss, relocation, divorce, the death of a loved one, serious illness or injury, and other stressful challenges—reveal that the ego is much more alive and well than we would prefer. How do we know this? Because our knee-jerk reaction is to resist these events. That's just human, you say? It is certainly characteristic of the human ego, but personal experience can reveal to us that the sooner we open, even if just barely, to the crisis as a teaching moment that holds something extremely important for us in the process of our evolution, the sooner we experience some relief, some opening, some spaciousness, some peace.

If we can practice opening to the crises in our personal lives as teaching moments, as evolutionary stepping stones, we will be far better prepared emotionally and spiritually for the trauma that collapse will foist on us and everyone around us.

In this manner, we enter hospice worker "training," which empowers us to accompany others, as well as ourselves, in "dying" to the values and assumptions of industrial civilization.

Moreover, it is important to make friends with literal death. How in the world do we do that in a culture that abhors the topic? I quote Duane Elgin from his article "Can Death Become Your Ally?"

> Death is an important ally for appreciating life. I am not refer-ring to a morbid preoccupation with death. Rather, I mean the felt awareness of our finitude as physical beings—an honest recogni-tion of the short time we have to love and to learn on this earth. The knowledge that our bodies will inevitably die burns through our attachments to the dignified madness of our socially con-structed existence. Death is a friend that helps us to release our clinging to social position and material possessions as a source of ultimate security and identity. An awareness of death forces us to confront the purpose and meaning of our existence, here and now (Huffington Post, July 3, 2011).

Contemplation of death is an integral part of the Buddhist tradition. Tibetan Buddhist monks often spend hours in a morgue just staring at dead bodies, and the Dalai Lama says he spends at least one hour a day contemplating his own death. While this may sound morbid, followers of this particular Buddhist tradition seem incredibly adept at creating joy in their lives. Perhaps that is because paradox is at the root of the tradi-tion—an acknowledgement that life and death travel together and cannot be separated from each other. To know death or to have had a near-death experience is to gain bone-marrow awareness of how precious life is. In order to thoroughly savor the life we live, it is necessary to make friends with death.

Protracted physical survival through the collapse will invariably result in countless encounters with physical death. It is safe to assume that entire neighborhoods, cities, regions, and countries will be annihilated over time. What will be most remarkable in that milieu will not be death, but survival. Those who survive will be the exception, not the rule, and in order to survive and retain some semblance of sanity, it will be necessary to befriend death and, at times, literally function as a hospice worker.

I watch my friend becoming a hospice worker for himself, and I watch myself becoming a hospice worker for him, and I watch both of us dancing at the threshold of life and death. I wonder to what extent in the collapse process I will become a hospice worker for other individuals, and to what extent others may become hospice workers for me. Meanwhile, I reflect on the words of Rumi.

Go die, O man of honor, before you die,
So that you will not suffer the pangs of death,
Die in such a way as to enter the abode of light,
Not the death that places you in the grave.

Every time we let go of some aspect of the old paradigm, the ego dies a bit more, and our deeper essence is revitalized. Each time we contemplate the limits of our mortality, the more capacity we have to focus on what matters right now and engage with life more fully. If you do not believe this is so, ask a person who has recently been diagnosed with a life-threatening illness or has recovered from one. Make death your ally in order to more passionately savor your life and to become a more skilled hospice worker for the world.

Getting Real about Our Predicament

A Climate Researcher on Collapsing Consciously

D r. Susanne Moser is a climate researcher at the University of California, Santa Cruz, and author of numerous articles on environmental leadership, including "Getting Real about It: Meeting the Psychological and Social Demands of a World in Distress." After discovering this article, I shared it far and wide, because it articulates so much of what I have been writing and teaching in all of my work. While the focus of the article is on environmental leadership, and although Moser casts this article in the light of climate change, it applies to all other global crises confronting our planet at this moment.

While grounded in hard science, Moser incorporates right-brain, intuitive exploration of the emotional and spiritual aspects of our predicament, not with an eye to providing us with a reassuring conclusion, but in order to compel us to "grow ourselves up," a notion emphasized by ecopsychologist, Bill Plotkin.

Consider this sobering quote from John Holdren, Obama's science advisor, cited from a 2010 issue of *The Economist*.

Facing the menace of growing, human-caused disruption of global climate, civilization has only three options: mitigation (taking steps to reduce the pace and the magnitude of the climatic changes we are causing); adaptation (taking steps to reduce the adverse impacts of the changes that occur); and suffering from impacts not averted by either mitigation or adaptation. We are already doing some of each and will do more of all, but what the mix will be depends on choices that society will make going forward. Avoiding increases in suffering that could become catastrophic will require large increases in the efforts devoted to both mitigation and adaptation.

In like manner, Moser notes that the choice we face is one between two kinds of transitions.

That then leaves us with two—or maybe only one-and-a-half—different scenarios for the future: one, in which we have done too little too late, resulting in our communities, economies, and the ecosystems we depend on being overwhelmed by the pace and magnitude of climate change, and all attendant losses and disruptions. In the transition to that future, we will experience a range of essential systems degrading over time, or collapsing outright, but in either case shifting into completely altered states. In the other scenario we will act—very soon and very fast—and thus experience radical changes in our energy, transportation, industrial and food systems, with deep implications for everything else we do—how and where we live, how and what we eat, how we get around, how we interact, how we work, and how we take care of our health and illnesses. In a span of merely a few decades we will decarbonize our lives completely. And while this happens, we will still experience significant impacts of climate change already set in motion from past emissions, and which we are committed to (lags in the system make the second scenario really just a modification of the first).

Obviously, the human species at large is in no way prepared for these scenarios. My work would not exist if it were, and my work *does* exist, because about five years ago I realized that someone must focus on emotional and spiritual preparation for confronting the consequences of our predicament in a world in which so few individuals are willing to "grow themselves up" and get real about what is so.

As stated above, Moser's focus in this article is on environmental leadership, and so she asks what it will mean to be an environmental leader in a collapsing world. She searches for the proper metaphor, "Be a steward, shepherd, arbiter, crisis manager, grief counselor, future builder?" Her answer is that the environmental leader will probably need to be all of these, and this is precisely what I have intended as I have consistently written and spoken about becoming an *elder*—a metaphor that arises from my affinity with indigenous traditions and the role of the elder as a steward of the culture on many levels.

As I have stated often, an elder is not necessarily an "older" but is mature enough to "get real" about what is so and to be the steward/ shepherd/arbiter/crisis manager/grief counselor/future builder—or whatever metaphor we may choose to describe people who have "grown themselves up" enough to face the truth of our predicament and utilize their gifts to be elders for the culture.

Moser quotes Bill McKibben, "We must accept the fact that the world we have known is going to change in hideous and damaging ways." When people first begin waking up, they often panic and want to fix the situation immediately by doing nothing in their lives but focusing fiercely on it. Rather, Moser suggests, "coming to grips with the reality we now are in takes time, and it is critical that we give it a quiet space inside ourselves, and that we ground ourselves in the face of it with any practices of balance we may already have or could adopt."

Here, this climate scientist is reemphasizing what I so doggedly asserted in *Navigating the Coming Chaos*, namely that we must build what I call our "internal bunker," developing our inner world in preparation for navigating our external one, and that we must work consciously and creatively with our human emotions to ground ourselves for interaction with a civilization in chaos. This takes time and commitment, and, yes, you may protest that we don't *have* the time. But I would ask, time for what? Time to save the world tomorrow? In the first place, the world can't be saved and certainly not tomorrow. Moreover, if you are genuinely "getting real," then you know that many more millions will die during and after collapse than will physically survive.

In fact, as Moser notes:

> The landscape you will find yourself in, once you allow this realization to take hold, is a different one. Despair lives there, along with helplessness and anger, fear and disorientation, undoubtedly also unspeakable sadness. You are likely to come to recognize that this is a new time. The time before was one in which we insisted and relied on hope, on better tomorrows, in the United States on the "American Dream." *Now, we have to accept that "better tomorrows" may not come. It is akin to accepting one's own mortality, maybe a doctor's prognosis of one's impending death, but on a much grander scale.* [my emphasis]

The moment we begin to consider our own mortality, we are in the territory of emotional and spiritual preparation for collapse, whether we want to go there or not. At that point, we need someone or something to help us navigate all the so-called negative emotions that surface, and we need support for finding and making meaning in every aspect of our lives.

Thus, after this section of her article, Moser immediately introduces "grief work," and I would add, work with fear, anger, and despair. What all of this is about is connecting with our deepest humanity and the deepest humanity of our fellow earthlings.

So we need to stop focusing on physical survival and focus instead on transition from the old paradigm to the new one. Why? Because, as Moser notes,

> The transition framing, with its inherent need to let go of the old, a time of the new not yet being formed, and the vision of a desirable outcome, this archetype of change provides us with a roadmap. Just having one will be a helpful thing. It sets an intention. It aids in recognizing markers along the way: the signs of decay, people's emotional reactions to it, experiments as seeds, the road

blocks and setbacks, the emergence of innovative ways that foster social, ecological, and cultural renaissance, and the specter of
an ending (even if it is beyond our own lifetime). Such a road-
map helps sustain the inordinate persistence, authentic hope, and
unprecedented commitment to moral action that will be required
of everyone even though the transition time is uncomfortable and
dangerous. It will evoke a very different kind of behavior than
merely "confronting collapse."

Moser asserts that we need to grow our capacity to be with our own
distress and to be with other people in distress. So often I have stated that
psychotherapy as we know it today will probably not exist in ten years
and that it is likely to be eclipsed by people coming together to engage in
deep listening and deep truth-telling.

Equally essential will be our ability to hold the tension of opposites.
Readers of my work are certainly familiar with that notion, articulated
beautifully here in the words of Dr. Moser:

> A logical concurrent demand then on future leaders will be to hold
> the paradoxes with which we all need to deal: with what is here and
> now and what could be globally and in the future; the distresses
> and joys in front of us and the possibilities of better or worse yet
> to come; the grief over what is being lost and the gratitude for
> what we still have; the fears that are inevitable and the hopes that
> we need; the practical realities of daily life and the vision of sys-
> temic change. In fact, a deliberate practice of visioning in the face
> of the unraveling will be a critically important practice.

Getting real about our predicament also means a willingness to
answer the call of leadership in helping to hammer out what Clinton Cal-
lahan calls "the next culture." For this reason, building one's isolated
doomstead or underground bunker is not only profoundly dangerous but
astoundingly unrealistic.

In *Navigating the Coming Chaos*, I emphasize that we cannot enter collapse consciously without deeply exploring our life purpose, our gifts, and our emotional landscape. Emotional and spiritual preparation is inextricably connected with questions we must ask: *Who do I want to be in the face of collapse? What did I come here to do?*

If you understand anything about collapse and are no longer living in denial, you are already an elder. The question is, Are you willing to claim that role and live your life purpose to the best of your ability in collapse? Are you willing to fully "grow yourself up"?

And thus, Susanne Moser concludes the article with this:

> There is nothing easy about the path of a true leader in these times. Accepting the responsibility of leadership will be a heavy burden, and those who take it on must help shape realistic expectations of what a leader can do. Clearly, this is not the kind of leadership that one takes on for the glory, the lure, and prestige of a top position. No one, not even the leaders, will have all the answers, and pretending to have them will be quickly unmasked. In the difficult times ahead, people may want quick and easy fixes, but what will sustain you and them are not flip answers, but quiet wisdom. Who, who indeed, will be those leaders? Inside you, a voice may make an answer to this question, to our ravenous, beautiful world (http://www.susannemoser.com/documents/Moser_chapter finaldraft_accepted.pdf).

A Culture of Two-Year-Olds and the Gifts of Collapse

Part 1

The only certainty regarding collapse is all of the uncertainty it holds. Will it be fast or slow? What to do about food, water, learning survival skills, relocation? One feels almost overwhelmed just thinking about all of the issues contained in the collapse of civilization, but perhaps none is as formidable as being forced to live very differently than we do now. Energy depletion and global economic crisis guarantee that the resources that fuel our current (rapidly becoming "former") American middle-class lifestyle will not be available. Peak oil means not only wildly fluctuating gas prices but skyrocketing prices for food and many other items that are now still affordable.

The Great Depression generation experienced shortages, and so will we, but Americans are unable to imagine the extent to which collapse will curtail their lifestyles. In fact, when I've raised these issues in classes or groups to which I've spoken, the responses have sometimes implied that the notion of having to limit one's consumption to such a severe extent is nothing less than un-American, echoing, once again, American exceptionalism and entitlement. Another frequent response, of course, is that I'm hopelessly negative and short sighted, because technology will always find a way out.

As a historian, I can freely use *exceptionalism* and *entitlement* to describe the attitudes above, but I was not always a historian. My training in psychology causes me to look into the deeper layers of an almost hysterical insistence that, as Americans, we shouldn't have to do without or be deprived. It's our inherent "right" to own SUVs, plasma TVs, and six-thousand-square-foot houses. Yet even those touting these "rights" know in some part of their psyches that their argument is irrational. If the majority of the earth's inhabitants cannot afford these things, then how can it be a "human right" or even an "American right" to insist on having them?

As Richard Heinberg states in *What a Way to Go: Life at the End of Empire,* "our culture has infantilized us to such an extent that we illogically assume and even demand that we must have our gas-guzzling vehicles and all of our other 'toys' that make an enormous energy footprint on the earth." Industrial civilization's refusal to accept limits has made humans not only self-absorbed, greedy, grasping, and "entitled," but it has also prevented them from developing the maturity to commit to leaving a sane and secure world to their children.

Few of us remember ourselves at the age of two, but most parents are quite familiar with two-year-old behavior. The two-year-old wants what she wants when she wants it, and her favorite word is "no!"—as long as she can *say* "no!" and doesn't have to be *told* "no!" At the age of two, children want to believe that they are omnipotent and have absolutely no limits. Their developmental task, however, is to be able to say "no" but also be able to accept the finality of being told "no." One of the reasons parents and psychologists refer to the twos as "terrible" is that caretakers must walk a fine line between allowing the child the right to say "no" but at the same time setting limits on the child's behavior.

The infantalization technique of industrial civilization is insidious in its ability to "hook" the two-year-old in us, deluding that part of us into believing that there are no limits and that we can have whatever we want—and not only that we *can* have it, but that we *should*. We prefer to be omnipotent with our money, our time, our environment, our relationships, and with most other aspects of life, but, ultimately, collapse will not permit us to be. For this reason, when fully in the throes of collapse, many individuals will feel abused, battered, persecuted, and victimized, and they will not experience the limits that collapse is setting on them as in their best interests. In fact, like children, they will look around for someone else to blame.

This is precisely what is happening in current time with the loose cannons of the Tea Party movement. They sense that something is wrong with the culture, as the psychic crisis of collapse exacerbates, but like tantruming two-year-olds, they seem incapable of advancing to an adult perspective that is large enough to make sense of their discomfort. Under the spell of the master manipulator Missionary Man, Glenn Beck, and entranced by the babbling beauty-queen bimbo, Sarah Palin, they eagerly consent to form the New Republic of Idiocracy—all facilitated by a massive dumbing down of American culture. All of their so-called analyses constitute sophomoric assessments that fail to comprehend the collapse of industrial civilization, and when, finally, they can no longer deny this reality, they will erupt even more violently in increasingly vitriolic scapegoating and belligerent attacks on those whom they myopically perceive as responsible for their plight.

Thus, those who understand collapse—why it is happening and that it *is* happening—and who, because they comprehend the finality of it, have been consciously preparing for it, will feel less victimized and will have more energy to actually participate positively in the experience of collapse.

While collapse brings hardship and sacrifice, it also brings opportunity. Those who are awake to it will be able to consciously navigate the landscape of transition. The omnipotent two-year-old, who formerly refused to accept limits, will have the option to grow up and become an adult who makes conscious choices about what will serve himself or herself, the community, and the earth.

Even as I have been called a "doomer" by those who do not understand the full spectrum of collapse, I have continued to insist that the news is not all bad. I see little indication from the progressive left and almost no indication from the conservative right or the center that they are willing to accept the limits that will be foisted on them by collapse. In fact, the notion that their lifestyles will be constrained by anything would strike them as profoundly absurd. Yet those who understand collapse also understand that such constraints are inherent in the process. Like an exasperated parent or a stern elder reining in a two-year-old, collapse will force unprecedented limits on the human race and compel a descent into the underworld of radical emotional and spiritual initiation. And as with indigenous initiations, the outcome is unknown, and there is never a guarantee that young women or men in tribal initiations will prevail instead of perish.

When I wrote *Sacred Demise* in 2008, I saw little evidence of a shift in consciousness in American culture. Today, while I still see cluelessness in command, I am also noticing more questioning, more openness to divergent perspectives, and more determination—particularly among young people—to forge a new path and a new way of being in the world. I suspect that many of them will be welcome allies for members of older generations weathering the storms of collapse.

My heart swells with excitement as I think of the individuals who are reading the signals, learning skills, relocating to more sustainable environments, and making the sacrifices collapse is demanding of our species. I imagine those who will, with reverence for the earth, grow glorious gardens; compost and recycle everything they possibly can; build beautifully designed natural habitats; make their own clothing and furniture; homeschool their children; build extraordinary, vibrant communities that serve and support one another; utilize herbal and other natural healing techniques; discover the joys of leisure spent with each other in a world where a power grid no longer exists, as people laugh, love, talk, make music, dance, tell stories, play, and commune with each other. Yes, perhaps all of this will occur against the backdrop of famine, pandemics, natural disasters, climate chaos, or even a nuclear exchange, and certainly not everyone will survive. Yet I am unwilling to forego the rebirth aspects of initiation, because they are always potentially present, without exception. As I've stated repeatedly, we all must hold the vision of rebirth alongside current reality in order to have an accurate picture of the whole.

Collapse is a form of death, and Americans do not like the word *death*. We go to extraordinary lengths to dress it up, prettify it, deny it, and—as my favorite of all meaningless anti-death clichés goes—"put it behind us." Like beasts of burden, we drive ourselves heroically in the first half of life as if there were no death. We believe that it will engulf others but not us. Remember, we are the "exception"; others will die, not us. Other civilizations will collapse, not ours. Yet it was Carl Jung who said that, "There is a great obligation laid upon the American people—that it shall face itself—that it shall admit its moment of tragedy in the present—admit that it has a great future only if it has the courage to face itself."

America, the nation, is not likely to face itself, but as individual earthlings, we must, if we intend to successfully navigate collapse. Part of me also resists collapse, for reasons similar to or different from those around me, but at the same time that I resist it, I am also consciously working to embrace it. To embrace something or someone is not necessarily to throw one's arms wildly around that event or person, but to slowly, intentionally open to the gifts inherent in what we most dread.

I do not say this lightly. I am a survivor of breast cancer. My world "collapsed" seventeen years ago, when I was diagnosed with it. But as is frequently the case, my world was also transformed by a possibly terminal illness, and I became a different person as a result of it. The Buddhist teacher Pema Chödrön writes, "Openness doesn't come from resisting our fears, but from getting to know them well." So what are the "gifts" of collapse?

First, collapse strips us of who we think we are, so that who we really are may be clearly revealed. Civilization's toxicity has fostered the illusion that one is, for example, a professional person with money in the bank, a secure mortgage, a good credit rating, and a healthy body and mind; that one is raising healthy children who will grow up to become successful in the same way; and that when one retires, one will be well taken care of. If that has become our identity, and if we don't look deeper, we won't discover who we really are, and as collapse intensifies, we will be shattered, because we have failed to notice the strengths, resources, and gifts that abide in our essence—all things that transcend and supersede our ego-identity.

In a post-collapse world, academic degrees and stock portfolios matter little. What really matters now is *who* is the person who has earned the degrees and accumulated the wealth? That person is a spiritual being, but also a human adult, and a real adult does not run from collapse but, rather, becomes intimately familiar with it.

A Culture of Two-Year-Olds and the Gifts of Collapse

Part 2

In his book *Nature and the Human Soul,* psychologist Bill Plotkin has provided us with a look at how differently humans might develop psychologically in an eco-centered, rather than an ego-centered, society. An ego-centered society serves the needs of industrial civilization and the consumption of its products, whereas in an eco-centered society, according to Plotkin, "its customs, traditions, and practices are rooted in an awareness of radical interdependence with all beings" (New World Library, 2008, 23). Thus, the crux of the tribal initiatory experience is the transformation of the childhood or adolescent ego into a fully developed, fully human individual who grasps wholly her interdependence and recognizes her purpose, that is, what she has come here to do.

One way to prepare for the initiatory experience of collapse is to explore the issue of identity apart from one's social roles. An individual may identify as an accountant, a teacher, an engineer, a therapist, but only in moments of solitude, away from the daily role of our profession, do we have the opportunity to explore who we really are. For me, a connection with something greater than the rational mind and human ego has been crucial in assessing who I am apart from what I do.

Second, collapse will decimate our anti-tribal, individualistic, Anglo-American programming by forcing us to join with others for survival. You may own a home outright, with ample acreage on which you have produced a stunning organic garden; you may have a ten-year cache of food and water, drive a hybrid car, and live a completely solarized life, but if you think you will survive in isolation, you are tragically deluded. Collapse dictates that we will depend on each other, or we will die.

I have been an activist for over thirty years. Without exception, every time I have been involved with other activists in promoting change, personalities clash, egos become bruised, some people throw tantrums, others become disillusioned and walk away from the group. We all seem to have PhDs in "self-sufficiency" but remain tragically ignorant of genuine cooperation. We will transform this pattern as civilization collapses, or we will perish, and the process of that transformation probably won't be pretty. However, we can begin preparing in present time for the collective thinking and action that collapse will necessitate by, for example, developing small support circles of community that meet regularly to engage in deep listening and truth telling about how we are experiencing collapse.

We will be compelled to relate differently not only to humans but to all beings in the nonhuman world as well. Only as we begin to read the survival manuals that trees, stars, insects, and birds have written for us will our species be spared. The very "pests" that we resent as unhygienic or annoying may, in fact, save our lives in the future. Three years ago, the honeybees used to circle around me on warm days when I ate my lunch outside, sitting on the grass under the trees. Two years later, as I sat under the same trees, on the same grass, the honeybees were gone. No one seems to be able to tell us why. Maybe it's time to ask the bees to tell us why.

Paradoxically, collapse may bring to our lives meaning and purpose that might otherwise have eluded us. In our linear, progress-based existence, we rarely contemplate words like "purpose." With civilization's collapse, we may be forced to evaluate daily, perhaps moment to moment, why we are here, if we want to remain here, if life is worth living, and if there is something greater than ourselves for which we are willing to remain alive and to which we choose to contribute energy. These decisions probably will not be made in the cozy comfort of our homes, but in the streets, the fields, the deserts, the forests, in the eerie echoing of our voices throughout abandoned suburbs, and beside forgotten rivers and trails.

Purpose will rapidly cease being about what we can accomplish and will increasingly become more about who we are. In a collapsing world, the so-called purpose-driven life will no longer exist. Humans will be "driven" by the determination to survive, to assist loved ones in surviving, and to plant the seeds of life lived in intimacy with the earth community. From that quest for survival and transformation will emerge authentic purpose, which will undoubtedly not resemble anything we can imagine today.

Lest the reader infer that I'm portraying collapse as some exercise in airy-fairy spirituality devoid of practicalities, I hasten to reemphasize what I have stated previously—that collapse will require humans to attend to the most pragmatic realities of existence—food, water, shelter, health care, and a host of other survival issues. As centralized systems such as federal, state, and local governments are eviscerated, communities will be compelled to unite if they have any hope of addressing these issues—to grow gardens, make clothing and other items, treat each other's illnesses, birth and bury one another, create community currencies, and rebuild infrastructures on an intensely local level. This will not be easy, and in the midst of feeling hopeless and fearful, it may feel impossible.

The quality of spirituality that may emerge from attending to the fundamentals may be an authentic "fundamentalism" in the truest sense of the word. In a post-collapse world, "fundamental" spirituality will be about caring for the basic needs of loved ones; becoming nurturing stewards of the ecosystem, in whatever condition it may be at that time; relearning what we value in the world—which won't be what was most important prior to collapse—seeing, hearing, smelling, tasting, feeling all aspects of existence to which we were oblivious or only mildly attentive before the distractions were stripped away. Certainly, this is not likely to be the comfortable, privileged, indulgent spirituality of the New Age workshop circuit but may more closely resemble the earth-based reverence for the sacred that our tribal ancestors demonstrated.

Spiritually, we can now begin preparing for the collapse of civilization as we have known it by opening ourselves each day to the "lesser collapses" of civilization that we see around us, such as the loss of a viable,

uncorrupted electoral process; the demise of centralized systems and corporations that no one ever thought would go bankrupt; the decay of infrastructure; and the deterioration of institutions such as education, religion,
health care, and the legal system. Human beings have been creating functional societies for thousands of years. Most of those civilizations have
also collapsed, because all civilizations ultimately do.

The United States has had more than two hundred years to fashion a
sustainable nation. But with the death of Abraham Lincoln at the end of
the Civil War, corporations and centralized systems triumphed in con-
trolling every aspect of American life, and they have been doing so until
the present moment. Thus, not surprisingly, in the 1970s, when corporate America knew very well that U.S. oil production had peaked and
that within three decades the nation and the world would be confronting
a catastrophic energy crisis, it did absolutely nothing. Instead, it chose
inebriation with the profits of hydrocarbon energy and the suppression
of alternative technology rather than assisting the nation in building life-
boats for navigating a post-petroleum world.

For millennia, many indigenous people have described the demise of
civilization we are now witnessing as a purification process—a time of
rebirth and transformation. Their ancient wisdom challenges us to face
with equanimity the collapse that is in process and to hold in our hearts
and minds—as much as humanly possible—the reality of the pain the
collapse will entail alongside the unimaginable opportunities it offers.

Some people tell me that they would rather not know what's going
on, because they prefer to live their lives from day to day, doing the best
they can to make a better world, enjoying their loved ones, and earning
their daily bread. I certainly understand their desire to protect themselves
from the pain of awareness, but I also know that they are exchanging
long-term preparedness for temporary comfort, and that the pain of
awareness in present time is far less than the pain they will incur as a
result of ignoring it.

I believe that here, at the end of the first decade of the twenty-first
century, none of us is facing collapse by accident. Our challenge is to
open to it with the awareness that it will bring gifts alongside adversity.

Once more I quote Pema Chödrön, whose words are remarkably appropriate: "Only with this kind of equanimity can we realize that no matter what comes along, we're always standing in the middle of sacred space. Only with equanimity can we see that everything that comes into our circle has come to teach us what we need to know."

PART 2

Transformative Truths
for Turbulent Times

Fifty-Two Weekly Meditations
on the Collapse of Industrial Civilization

*When the horror recedes and the world resumes its normal shape, you
cannot forget it. You have seen what is "really" there, the empty horror that exists when the consoling illusion of our mundane experience is
stripped away, so you can never respond to the world in quite the same
way again.*

KAREN ARMSTRONG

*We live in radical times surrounded by tasks that seem impossible. It has
become our collective fate to be alive in a time of great tragedies, to live
in a period of overwhelming disasters and to stand at the edge of sweep-
ing changes. The river of life is flooding before us, and a tide of poisons
affect the air we breathe and the waters we drink and even tarnish the*

dreams of those who are young and as yet innocent. The snake-bitten condition has already spread throughout the collective body.

However, it is in troubled times that it becomes most important to remember that the wonder of life places the medicine of the self near where the poison dwells. The gifts always lie near the wounds, the remedies are often made from poisonous substances, and love often appears where deep losses become acknowledged. Along the arc of healing the wounds and the poisons of life, are created the exact opportunities for bringing out all the medicines and making things whole again.

MICHAEL MEADE, *Fate and Destiny*

1

This we have now
Is not imagination.

This is not
grief or joy.

Not a judging state,
Or an elation,
Or sadness.

Those come
and go.

This is the presence
that doesn't.

RUMI

What is the "presence" of which Rumi speaks? Words sometimes used synonymously are the *sacred*, *spirit*, the *transcendent*. All suggest the nearness of something greater than the rational mind and the human ego. In this excerpt from one of Rumi's longer poems, he assures us that the presence is eternal and never falters—and never leaves. Whatever our feeling state, our mental preoccupation, or our physical condition, whether we are aware of the presence or not, it remains. The presence is always with us, even in the current unraveling and even if we are only sometimes with the presence.

We can consciously connect with the presence through meditation, through intentional engagement with nature, or by allowing ourselves to experience beauty through art, music, poetry, or other forms of creative expression in which we allow beauty to touch and inspire us. We cannot control our experience of presence, but we may ask it to visit us, and we can open to however it manifests. Like the biblical Jacob, who, wrestling with the angel, cried out, "I will not let you go until you bless me," we must be willing to *be* present with the presence. When we are fully open, we may be astonished by the gift of presence—a gift by which we are infused with gratitude and humility.

Will you take time today to be present with presence? All else comes and goes, but the presence does not.

2

The excessive emphasis on the fast-paced instant way of life is undoubtedly the most dangerous enemy of joy. As much as possible, as fast as possible, its motto. It leads to more and more fun and less and less joy.
HERMANN HESSE

The culture of modernity does not know joy. It knows obsession with technology, instant messaging, theme parks, extreme sports, NASCAR racing, video gaming, and sky diving—all of which have allowed us to drown ourselves in fun, but for the most part, joy eludes us.

Joy is very different from happiness, fun, or entertainment. It is related to the Latin *gaudere,* "to rejoice." Both "joy" and "rejoice" have spiritual undertones that suggest a sense of gratitude. Whenever we are grateful, a relationship of some sort is implied. We give thanks, but to whom or to what? Certainly not to ourselves.

To rejoice means "to take delight in," which suggests an experience far deeper and more penetrating for the soul than mere happiness. In reality, one can experience joy even in the midst of sorrow—as a friend of mine, now recovering from battling cancer and surviving a stem-cell transplant, frequently reminds me. In the throes of his cancer ordeal, my friend often said, "This is so horrible, but I feel so much joy as I walk this path consciously." And perhaps that is the pivotal difference between happiness and joy. One can be "happy" and be astonishingly unconscious, but joy demands awareness, gratitude, and being present in the body.

Curiously, the word *joy* is related to the Spanish word for jewel, *joya*. Thus it would seem that to experience joy and to know that one is experiencing it is like holding a precious jewel throughout the vicissitudes of the human condition, so often fraught with sorrow, disappointment, and loss. In order to consciously feel and savor joy, however, it is necessary to slow down and mindfully attend to our experience from moment to moment. No matter how much elation or stimulation a fast-paced lifestyle brings us, it is ultimately, as Hesse reminds us, the enemy of joy.

3

To be alive in this beautiful, self-organizing universe—to participate in the dance of life with senses to perceive it, lungs that breathe it, organs that draw nourishment from it—is a wonder beyond words.

JOANNA MACY

No matter how daunting your life may feel in this moment, these words are no less true than if you were experiencing a state of ecstasy. For many people who are living through incalculable losses, this sentence may be all they have to hold on to in some moments of their anguish.

Whatever we *don't* have in this moment, we have our bodies. Perhaps our bodies are not as healthy as they could be, and we may even need health care that we can't afford, but the systems of the body still operate. If you are reading these words, you still have lungs that breathe and organs that function. Both are miracles that you can stop and contemplate right now.

If you are able to walk in nature, I suggest a gratitude walk or hike. It should be done in silence, as you slowly, deeply reflect on everything you encounter for which you are grateful. What gifts, surprises, insights, joys, or challenges offer themselves to you on this excursion?

If you can't walk, then look around and deeply contemplate the blessings in your surroundings. Which ones have you previously overlooked? Which are the dearest and most precious? Why?

As Brother David Steindl-Rast notes in his wonderful book *Gratefulness, the Heart of Prayer*, regardless of our spiritual path or the absence of one, when we express gratitude, we are acknowledging either human forces or the power of something greater—or both. We may "take something for granted" not realizing that, indeed, it has been "granted." Therefore, consciously feeling or expressing gratitude is humbling, which may be one reason some individuals rarely do so. Nevertheless, in that very humility lies unimaginable liberation and aliveness.

Depression may be rampant around us, but it is impossible to feel depressed at the same time that one feels grateful. Moods come and go, and we may have little emotional or chemical control over them, but feeling and expressing gratitude are choices, and they can punctuate and temper dark emotional states.

4

To be in a body is to hear the heartbeat of death at every moment.
ANDREW HARVEY

All around us, death. People dying, systems dying, nature dying, lifestyles dying, dreams dying. How do we persevere? Constant reminders of our own mortality that evoke the question, how much longer do I have?

Why does the Dalai Lama spend an hour a day contemplating his own death? Why do some Buddhist monks spend hours staring at dead bodies? The poet Rumi tells us, "die before you die." But what does that mean?

For several years I have included in my workshops an exercise that guides participants in imagining, very graphically, their own death. I am aware of other workshop facilitators who have used similar processes. I rarely let participants know ahead of time that we will be doing this exercise. Almost without exception, however, after people have experienced it, they tell me that that exercise alone was worth the price of admission.

One reason for including this process is to directly address the fear of death that hides behind our denial of collapse, our insistence that civilization isn't really collapsing or that, if it does, a million wonderful opportunities will emerge to make it all worthwhile. Once we get our fear of death in full view and no longer on the back burner—once we deal with the reality of our death, consciously and unequivocally, alongside others in a group—a profound shift occurs, and we can stop denying collapse or any other demise in the human experience.

Contemplating our mortality on a daily, if not hourly, basis is a very useful practice, both in turbulent times and in tranquil times. Not only does it support a reordering of our priorities, it reminds us that we are not the ego. The deeper self, our true essence, is eternal and unchanging. A 1960s Beatles song sung by John Lennon says, "Nothin's gonna change my world."

By this, Lennon did not mean that the external world would not change, but that the sacred Self is constant, eternal, untouched by the relative world of ego and thought forms. Listen regularly to the heartbeat of death.

5

When the dark times come around and the end seems near again, it becomes more essential for the individual person to learn and live the story the soul carries from before birth.

MICHAEL MEADE, *The World Behind the World*

Original Instructions

One way to connect with the other-inner-under world is through the story the soul carries. Pondering that story—the story of our lives, its many twists and turns of fate, and the parts that remain to be played out—all of these offer clues regarding our fate and destiny and what it is we came here to do.

I notice in Michael Meade's statement the words, "when . . . the end seems near again." This implies that we have experienced many endings before—just as the world has experienced many endings in the past. We have all died hundreds, if not thousands, of "little" deaths in our lifetimes. But an ending is always the beginning of something, even though it is sometimes difficult to discern where one thing ends and another begins.

The ending of industrial civilization is also the beginning of what some have called "the next culture." Thus, we are all part not only of this ending but of the new beginning, the new culture that is attempting to emerge. Yet it will not simply emerge; it needs human midwives and architects. The story of industrial civilization is rapidly ending, and the next culture desperately needs new stories. Paradoxically, however, those new stories must be written by returning to the ancient stories of indigenous people before the advent of industrial civilization.

The words *culture* and *cultivate* have a common root, and living with ancient stories, myths, and fairy tales alongside a conscious, soul-centered deciphering of our own personal story is one of the most meaningful ways of both cultivating a rich inner life and creating a new culture. Turbulent times are ideal times for discovering the synchronicity between the two. An extraordinary opportunity to discover the world behind the world—a world that never ends—informing all of the ends and beginnings of the chaotic and troubled world we currently inhabit.

6

Freedom is the ultimate spiritual longing of an individual human being, but freedom is only appreciated when it falls within the parameters of a larger sense of belonging.

DAVID WHYTE

With the unraveling of society and culture, we may experience many real or imagined threats to our freedom. Laws and their enforcement may break down. Systems may disintegrate and become ash heaps of former modernity. As governments on life support attempt to maintain control and legitimacy, they may become increasingly totalitarian. Or in more remote areas, where the long arm of the law may have been severely shortened by economic collapse, certain individuals may usurp control in opportunistic attempts to enhance their own survival opportunities. On the other hand, the collapse of larger systems may result in more freedom than many of us could have imagined—at least for a while. But nature abhors a vacuum, and the absence of civic structure may ultimately result in severe repression.

Whatever freedom we experience—or not—it is wise to remember David Whyte's words regarding "the parameters of a larger sense of belonging." Industrial civilization has put many of us into exile—from ourselves, from the community, and from nature. Now we have the opportunity and, I believe, the necessity of discovering what it means to belong. Without community, we will not survive these turbulent times. With community, it is possible to experience a new level of safety, support, and thriving beyond mere survival. For many, this will be their very first experience of belonging since childhood—or, perhaps, ever.

We may not love everyone in our community or revel in their companionship, but belonging is a human need that must be met in challenging times if we are to navigate the pitfalls of collapse and value our existence in the messy remnants of what was once a thriving civilization. When we experience healthy parameters of belonging, we are truly free. The old paradigm argues that it is only the independent "free spirit" who has full liberty to be himself or herself. Do we need to look any further to see where this old story has gotten us?

7

There's a thread you follow. It goes among
things that change. But it doesn't change.
WILLIAM STAFFORD

Perhaps nothing in these turbulent times is more urgent than our awareness that the thread lives within us and that we feel its presence in our lives. In times of dizzying and daunting change, the thread remains, always available for us to touch and pluck, and in so doing, we feel our connection with ancestors, ancient wisdom, timeless truth, and the eternal remnants of the sacred.

Our work is not only to hold on to the thread, but to use it to reweave and remake our world with the unraveling fibers of a garment we inherited from the Enlightenment—a garment that eventually became a smothering weight upon our souls and a blanket of seduction and sorrow.

While we hold the thread, Stafford assures us, we can't get lost. Things fall apart; people question our choices, perhaps even conclude that we are insane. Yet we hold on to the thread and help our fellow human beings find theirs. When we feel overwhelmed, we hang on to the thread, and when our neighbor is near succumbing to madness, we offer a poem, a song, a story, or something beautiful to soothe and soften the terror—something that will remind him of the thread he hasn't found but has never lost. As we cherish the thread, we increasingly understand how intimately we are all woven together in a garment called *life*. In fact, that is what turbulent times have always taught humans.

8

Each person searches for his life task before he is born.
But how do we find out what this life goal is?
When a woman is pregnant a ritual is performed, called the listening
*   ritual. In this ritual the Elders of the village ask the unborn child:*
Who are you?
Where do you come from?
Why are you taking the trouble to come into this messed up world? What
*   can we do to make your journey easier?*
   SOBONFU SOMÉ, *The Gift of Happiness*

In *Entering the Healing Ground*, Francis Weller speaks of "spiritual employment," a term that refers to the gifts that each of us carries in our soul when we enter this life. Sobonfu Somé, of the Dagara tribe of West Africa, speaks of the importance of the community knowing what each child is bringing, so the village can support him or her.

In this time of massive unemployment, a time that may signal the end of the full-time job as we have known it, it is becoming increasingly important for us to know what gifts we have brought into the world and what we really came here to do—beyond any job that we may have or have had in the past.

In *Fate and Destiny,* Michael Meade suggests that one reason we have become a consumer society is that we have lost the connection with our inherent gifts and, in so doing, have found our identity in consumption, thus becoming spiritually unemployed. If, in building the next culture, we are to forsake our identity as consumers, we must find our authentic identity, which can only be discovered in the awareness of our gifts. For, as Meade says, "In becoming aware of one's natural gifts the need to give something to the world becomes stronger than the hunger to consume it."

The elders are stewards and protectors of the culture. Their role is not defined by age but by the wisdom they have developed through personal and cultural initiations. In the next culture, elders must work with the community to discover the gifts in each person, just as each person must work to discover those gifts in himself or herself. In this way, we become midwives of the soul, assuring that our community will sustain full spiritual employment.

9

There is a brokenness out of which comes the unbroken
A shatteredness out of which blooms the unshatterable.
There is sorrow beyond all grief which leads to joy,
And a fragility out of whose depths emerges strength.
RASHANI

Who could not spend years contemplating these words? And perhaps you will. As I linger with Rashani's words, my body reverberates with her exquisite juxtaposition of light and dark, sorrow and joy, brokenness and wholeness, fragility and strength. Surely, these lines from her extraordinary poem are especially suited for turbulent times—the poet holds in her heart and articulates through her pen a union of opposites that resonates with all that we know to be true at our core.

As we sit with the anguish around us—or, perhaps, in our own lives—some part of us is aware that it is not the whole truth, the entire story. In the deep recesses of the psyche, we sense that collapse, unraveling, demise, and chaos represent only one half of what is trying to happen to us and our species. The ancient alchemists understood that by patiently staying present to both the fire and the lead in the alchemical container, the baser metal could and would be transmuted into gold. They also understood that the process was an arduous, wrenching, agonizing ordeal—that it could never occur effortlessly, without painstaking, unswerving commitment.

Holding the tension of opposites—demise and creativity, violence and tenderness, blight and beauty, death and rebirth—is the most difficult and sometimes heartbreaking work any human can do. Yet this is what is being asked of us at this juncture of our species' history. Our souls are being torn asunder, and still—and unequivocally—we are learning to sing.

10

Crisis is the time for truth.
CHELLIS GLENDINNING

The collapse of industrial civilization will compel us to do and not do many things, but above all, it will compel us to tell the truth—the truth about our environment, our natural resources, our use and misuse of money, our disconnection from the earth community—and above all, it will compel us to tell the truth about ourselves.

With intensifying collapse comes a radical reordering of values and priorities. How so many things that mattered before now matter little. How urgently crucial in this moment is so much that we previously disregarded or minimized. But beyond all of that, we are being confronted with who we really are, not the image that we have been driven to portray.

So much is being revealed now, and that is precisely what the word *apocalypse* originally meant: the unveiling. Every institution, as it disintegrates, is being revealed for what it has become. And each of us is and will be "unveiled" as the rigors of the unraveling intensify.

Pretense is over; there's nowhere to run, nowhere to hide. We cannot afford to say anything but what is so, and if we attempt to do otherwise, our untruth will be revealed. Time to tell the truth about the old paradigm. Time to tell the truth about how it has murdered our souls, because only radical truth telling can restore our souls and allow us to reclaim our wholeness.

Crisis separates the wheat from the chaff, because it reveals what is true or untrue, and perhaps that is its most painful and unanticipated result. We say we don't want to lose a way of life to which we have become accustomed, because it is comfortable and familiar, but perhaps the deeper truth is that we are frightened that when we do lose it, the truth of who we are will be irrevocably exposed. Denial and delusion hide our warts, but they also conceal the authentic gold of the sacred Self. We must structure and steward a new paradigm, at the heart of which is the inexorable reality of both the warts and the gold.

11

Love animals. God has given them the rudiments of thought and joy untroubled. Do not trouble their joy, don't harass them, don't deprive them of their happiness, don't work against God's intent. Man, do not pride yourself on superiority to animals, they are without sin, and you, with your

*greatness, defile the earth by your appearance on it, and leave the traces of
your foulness after you—alas, it is true of almost every one of us!*
Fyodor Dostoyevsky

One of the most tragic victims of turbulent times is the more-than-human world. So many millions are casualties of economic collapse; extreme weather disasters; neglect; and calculated, vicious abuse. Almost all pain and suffering among animals is in some way connected with humanity's pride and sense of superiority toward them.

Animals have two attributes that humans have great difficulty attaining. They are totally and completely in their bodies, and they do not have egos. This makes for a creature that is thoroughly present and often able to navigate an uncertain world with a stealthy grace uncommon to humans.

In grueling economic times, I believe that we must help protect the most vulnerable among us: children, the elderly, and the animals. Very difficult choices may confront us in terms of who we choose to feed or not feed. It may be extremely difficult or even impossible to care for all the animals we encounter, and as animal shelters and other safety-net organizations become increasingly rare—or even become nonexistent—the likelihood of keeping our hearts open toward the plight of animals could prove to be overwhelming.

We can only do our best to act with love and compassion, and we can allow each being we encounter to be a teacher. Some of the greatest teachers on earth are our brothers and sisters from the more-than-human world. Open yourself to the love, wisdom, stealth, and body presence of the animals. Become a student of the creatures who navigate the world with their bodies, senses, and instincts. Celebrate your animal body and soul. Work with, not against, God's intent.

12

One day Nasrudin was walking along a deserted road. Night was fall-ing as he spied a troop of horsemen coming toward him. His imagina-tion began to work, and he feared that they might rob him, or impress him into the army. So strong did this fear become that he leaped over a wall and found himself in a graveyard. The other travelers, innocent of any such motive as had been assumed by Nasrudin, became curious and pursued him.

When they came upon him lying motionless, one said, "Can we help you? And, why are you here in this position?"

Nasrudin, realizing his mistake said, "It is more complicated than you assume. You see, I am here because of you; and you, you are here because of me."

SUFI TALE

The teachings and folklore of Sufi mysticism are replete with quotes and jokes from Nasrudin. I have included this joke because one of the most important and salutary practices during turbulent times is laughter. No matter how daunting our days and nights may be, we must repeatedly return to laughter, because darkness cannot exist without light. No matter how bleak our world may be, we must create both beauty and laughter.

We know with certainty that even in Nazi death camps, inmates found occasions for laughter and joke telling. Death, loss, horror, cruelty, and dissolution are not the entire story of the human condition. Equally real are moments of laughter, joy, fun, play, and giddiness. Not only do we need laughter for balance and as a tonic for the soul, we need it for the veracity of our experience. That is to say, if we lose our souls in suffering, we are living only part of the reality of industrial civilization's collapse and, therefore, living a half-truth.

Some years ago, a friend of mine spoke about "inflicting" joy on others. At some point, every occasion provides an opportunity for us to inflict joy, and naturally, we must be discreet and tactful in doing so. In a world of loss and painful transition, laughter is desperately needed. When we laugh, the mind and the ego recede, and we join the soul and the souls of others in celebrating our circulation in the soup of life.

How can you inflict joy on your world today?

13

Two prisoners whose cells adjoin communicate with each other by knock-ing on the wall. The wall is the thing which separates them but is also their means of communication. It is the same with us and God. Every separation is a link.

SIMONE WEIL, activist in the French Resistance,
World War II

We have entered a time in human history in which every person, every event, every experience compels us to fully and finally grasp that the separation between ourselves and others does not exist. Even the walls we construct between ourselves and others—the resent-ments, fears, jealousies, all of our defenses—keep us connected, albeit in distorted ways, but nevertheless connected with those we seek to push away.

Inherent connectedness may be the overarching lesson that humanity is being asked to learn in this time of upheaval. We cannot terminate our connection with anyone or anything, even in death. Knowing this may be extremely useful in situations where it is not feasible to connect directly with someone—if the person has shut us out of his or her life, or if there has been some other rupture between us. In fact, we can sit quietly, enter a place of deep stillness inside, and allow our sacred Self to silently speak to the sacred Self of the other person. We do this not to justify or explain ourselves, but to acknowledge our infinite, interminable oneness with that individual. In the domain of recognizing our oneness with the other in deep stillness, miracles often happen. Journaling and writing letters that we will not send are also useful in certain situations, because they open our hearts and allow unrecognized awarenesses to surface.

Literal, concrete connections with estranged or dead loved ones, friends, or foes may not be possible in real time, but neither is total psychic disconnection. Every separation is a link.

14

You don't get to vote on what is. Have you noticed?
BYRON KATIE

In the good times of economic prosperity, it was easier to live in denial. After all, we could reach for the alcohol, the food, the credit card, or the next love interest and for a while, make it all go away. When times are tough, when, perhaps, we aren't even sure where the next meal is coming from, we are smitten with what is. We choose either to reach for yet another soporific or to sit still and stare down what is.

Refusal to face what is, is intimately connected with living somewhere else besides the present moment. Maybe if I can just be somewhere else, I can escape what is. Yet, as the saying goes, wherever you go, there you are.

For all the bad press denial receives, it does have a survival function in the human psyche. Without denial, all of us would have been driven to madness long ago, but most of us have failed to view it as a defense mechanism and chosen instead to use it as a first response to anything unpleasant in our world. Materialism, addiction to technology, and a sense of entitlement have a way of encouraging us to do exactly that. And we usually embrace denial because we lack the tools that empower us to confront what is.

Whatever your situation in this moment, you cannot escape what is. This may be one of the hidden blessings in the collapse of industrial civilization. So many of the things we have utilized in the past to buffer and create distance from what is will be less available or, perhaps, not available at all. Denial is a childlike state in which we refuse to grow up and become mature adults with the capacity to confront what is. These turbulent times are not just nudging us to evolve but, in some cases, kicking us in the pants to force us to forsake denial and tell ourselves and the world the truth about the plight of our planet.

I suspect that most people reading these words are doing so because they have long ago realized that they have no vote on what is, even if they are still engaged in a protracted struggle with denial. None of us, no matter how informed or evolved, is ever completely devoid of denial. Where are the last vestiges of denial in you? In what ways might you subtly be trying to have a vote on what is?

15

I don't recall ever feeling this awake.
        THELMA, in *Thelma and Louise*

One of his students asked Buddha, "Are you the messiah?"
    "No," answered Buddha.
    "Then are you a healer?"
    "No," Buddha replied.
    "Then are you a teacher?" the student persisted.
    "No, I am not a teacher."
    "Then what are you?" asked the student, exasperated.
    "I am awake," Buddha replied.

Is there really a difference between Thelma and Buddha? A man named Siddhartha grows up in the warrior caste of his country and abdicates all privilege, choosing instead to become a monk and commit his life to ending suffering. A law-abiding, subservient woman becomes unintentionally entangled in a maelstrom of crime and finds herself sitting in a car beside her accomplice on a starry night, declaring that she's "crossed a line" and will never go back to her former life. Both the man, Siddhartha, and the woman, Thelma, declare that they are awake.

There are as many ways to awaken as there are human beings on earth, and there is no one "right" way. Some of us awaken early in our lives, others awaken late, perhaps too late to survive turbulent times. In a chaotic world, we are surrounded by people who are in various stages of awakeness and befuddlement. While it is never too late to awaken, it may be too late to make the changes in our lives and our world that we would have preferred to make. Nevertheless, I would argue that it is better to awaken too late than not at all.

We cannot be awake and simply revel in our awakeness. Action is an inevitable result of becoming conscious. If you feel awake, what is your awakeness calling you to? For Thelma, awakeness ultimately called her to death. For Buddha, the call was to end suffering. Take time to contemplate and savor your awakening process. Are you committed to continuing that process? If so, how? And what action has been born from your awakening? What further action might be gestating and waiting to emerge, even as you read these words?

16

The shadow is a moral problem that challenges the whole ego-personality, for no one can become conscious of the shadow without considerable moral effort. To become conscious of it involves recognizing the dark aspects of the personality as present and real. This act is the essential condition for any kind of self-knowledge.

CARL JUNG

We owe an enormous debt to Jung for defining and articulating the concept of the shadow. Essentially, the shadow is any part of us that we disown and say is "not me." For example, we may say of the liar, "That's not me, I always tell the truth," yet some part of us is not fully honest. Likewise, we may disavow the most loathsome qualities that we see around us as "not me." Stealing, cheating, infidelity, avarice, envy, duplicity, opportunism, hate, violence—all of these we insist are "not me," yet all of these exist in the psyche of every human being, whether or not she is conscious of them.

While this may feel depressing to contemplate, Jung assured us that 80 percent of the shadow is "pure gold." What did he mean? Simply that if we are willing to confront the shadow in ourselves and work with it, that work can profoundly transform us and lead us into intimate contact with the sacred Self. Moreover, when we persevere in working with the shadow, the experience of joy is inevitable.

Our work is to allow the ego to open sufficiently so that parts of the shadow can be seen. While we may not have the key to the door behind which the shadow is locked, we can drill a few holes in the walls to permit just enough light to enter that the shadow may be seen. We may feel disgust as we begin viewing the shadow, but we may also gradually notice a feeling of compassion for it and for the wounding that engendered it. Confronting the shadow is an intensely humbling experience for the ego and, in some cases, perhaps even shattering.

Yet we will never discover the largeness or largess of the sacred Self until we have allowed ourselves to see and weep for the shadow. Rumi wrote, "There is a shredding that's really a healing, that makes you more alive." The gold in doing shadow work is not only more aliveness but more compassion for our fellow earthlings who have not yet found the gold within themselves.

17

It is no measure of health to be well adjusted to a profoundly sick society.
JIDDU KRISHNAMURTI

How many years have you spent *not* adjusting to industrial civilization? Perhaps you didn't know you were doing that, and perhaps you had no words for how you were choosing to live your life. But as the world crisis worsened, the awareness that you were not conforming to the infinite growth paradigm, the mindless use of energy, and humanity's mass extinction of every species, including itself—all of that—may have revealed to you how sick your world had become.

Or perhaps you did not question your society's values until you had lost a job, a home, retirement savings, health insurance, or something else you believed would never go away. At that point you may have begun to look at your society with new eyes, and in connecting the dots, you may have discovered the sickness therein.

Whatever your history of awakening, it may be that you now understand that in the next culture, "adjustment" must be supplanted by accountability, and "conformity" by genuine community. In that new milieu, humans should be welcome *not* to adjust, and the community must be willing to listen to and dialog with all who challenge it. In the crucible of community, utilizing the tools of conscious communication, we have the possibility of making and remaking the next culture. Moreover, I believe that the very anguish of collapse will facilitate this process. For it may be that the deeper the suffering, the more committed to creating whole societies of whole human beings we will be.

In any event, the next culture must not have a dominant paradigm to which everyone must conform; it must be forged by individuals who include and value the ideas and talents of everyone. In other words, what must be prized is not conformity but creativity.

18

Finding beauty in a broken world is creating beauty in the world we find.
TERRY TEMPEST WILLIAMS

In a declining environment, it is sometimes difficult to find beauty, particularly in areas where a great deal of blight or decay exists. Much of nature has been ravaged by humans or by human-created climate change. Depending on where one lives, it may be challenging to access natural beauty. Whereas in the past we may have relied on walks in the forest as a way of immersing ourselves in natural beauty, those forests may now be gone or severely altered. We may be used to a melodious sound system or regular attendance at the symphony for experiencing beautiful music, which won't be available in the future. Movies, plays, and art galleries may no longer be accessible in a changed world. We will no longer be able to depend on technology as a conduit to beauty.

Consequently, if we are going to find and create beauty, we will need to lower our techno-embellished expectations and return to the most simplistic ways of doing so—ways with which our ancestors were intimately familiar. Finding and creating beauty may be as uncomplicated as observing a blade of grass that has burst through concrete or watching a sparrow peck meticulously at bread crumbs we have thrown it. Or we may experiment with hollowing out a branch or reed into which we carve holes to make a flute. The music of beautiful wind chimes can easily be provided by scavenging all manner of materials just lying around in piles of rubble.

As the world becomes more blighted and even more brutal, savoring and creating beauty becomes a sacred act. In doing so, we affirm that the most distasteful aspects of our species and external world do not have the last word—that something else more radiant within the human soul still prevails. That "something" is the capacity to revere beauty, natural or otherwise. Yet another statement by Terry Tempest Williams underscores our connection with beauty and beauty's relationship with our sacred universe: "The world is holy. We are holy. All life is holy. Daily prayers are delivered on the lips of breaking waves, the whisperings of grasses, the shimmering of leaves."

19

An elder sitting in the back of the room at a Native American council group has authority. Not because he holds a higher rank, but because he has certain values.

JAMES HILLMAN

Our ancient ancestors were tribal people, which, by definition, meant that their structure was communal rather than hierarchical. Many tribes were matriarchal societies in which matrons or clan mothers had ultimate authority. For example, among the Iroquois Confederacy of early North America, men needed permission from the clan mothers to go to war.

For most of the ancients, one's life journey centered around ultimately becoming an elder of the tribe. Elderhood was not based on political authority but on one's depth of wisdom. Today, we choke on information but starve for wisdom. For them, wisdom meant, as Michael Meade states, learning to extract living knowledge from the struggles of life, all of which led them to develop profound insight into their own lives. In other words, a descent into the depths of life is required in order to develop wisdom. Authentic elders act as a bridge between this world and the other world, and, according to Meade, the word *weird* was synonymous with *elder* in some ancient societies. *Weird* simply meant having one foot in each world. Weirdness and wisdom were closely related.

As we aspire to be elders in a culture in decay and a world unraveling, it is crucial to have one foot in this world and one in the other world. While that may appear weird to many of our peers, it is our calling at this moment in time. We must have one foot firmly on the ground of survival and the other in the realm of the soul, the sacred Self. That posture may feel more distressingly weird to us than to anyone else, but it is only that stance that qualifies us for elderhood and thus equips us to steward, with great inner *authority* (related to the word *authentic*), a world in which the *in*-authentic structures of the human ego agonize in abject decay.

Are we willing to persevere in this descent so that we gain the capacity to access the deeper wisdom that flows from mining the gold at the soul's center?

20

The spirit is fascinated by the future, wants to know the meaning of everything, and would like to stretch, if not break altogether, the laws of nature through technology or prayer. It is full of ideals and ambition, and is a necessary, rewarding, and inspiring aspect of human life.

The soul is . . . embedded in the details of ordinary, everyday experience. In the spirit we try to transcend our humanity; in the soul, we try to enter our humanity fully and realize it completely.

THOMAS MOORE, *The Education of the Heart*

From the moment I began writing about the collapse of industrial civilization, in the early years of this century, I have been asked to predict how collapse will unfold. I have always resisted stating specifics but have certainly been willing to articulate the general patterns we have been witnessing.

At this moment, we do not know how much more dire or daunting collapse will prove to be. I firmly believe that in order for our species to experience an evolutionary leap, we must first hit bottom. What will be required for that to occur, I cannot say. What I can say is that circumstances are likely to become much worse than they presently are.

Whenever I receive the linear inquiry regarding what will happen next, I attempt to shift the emphasis from future to present. On the one hand, I have adamantly asserted for many years that we must prepare for the future, but I am still a firm advocate for the value of staying embodied in the present moment. For at least the past three hundred years, industrial civilization has seduced us into being somewhere besides in our bodies in the present moment—into transcending the dark realities of the human condition with notions of exceptionalism, entitlement, and unfathomable denial.

What the soul wants, conversely, is for us to be grounded, embodied, and fully here, that is to say, fully human. What might happen to us if we allow this? What might we become? What might small communities of humans who are committed to becoming fully embodied and fully human be able to achieve in the coming century? This is the kind of future forecasting I prefer—not one in which we engage in cerebral prognostication about how collapse will unfold, but heartful envisioning of how we will be remade by what it is asking of us: to embrace the deepest layers of our humanity and physicality and realize them completely.

21

You have come to the shore. There are no instructions.
Denise Levertov

So here we are, living in times we may have never dreamed possible, at least for us, with our secure job, solid education, fixed-rate mortgage, and the many creature comforts for which we worked so hard. We are now in waters for which few of us have received formal training. Even the courses we may have taken in permaculture design, organic gardening, woodworking, emergency response, or nonviolent communication could never have fully prepared us for the collapse of all institutions, global resource evaporation, climate chaos, and the degree of frugality forced upon us by economic meltdown.

Are we really supposed to make it all up as we go along? In fact, our ancestors did just that on millions of occasions. Whether it was our recent ancestors who cleared the forests of the New World or our distant ancestors who discovered what could happen when sparks from the friction of two sticks rubbed together ignited the grass, the history of our species is the history of surrender to what wasn't working, and openness to what might.

All of the great wisdom traditions and the sages whose words are recorded in this book would remind us that we are not alone. Not having instructions does not mean that we have no help. Great things have often been accomplished by people who felt abjectly helpless and unskilled.

The shore is a terrifying *and* exciting place to be.

Never underestimate the power of willingness, openness to asking the sacred Self for assistance, and connection with others who feel similarly adrift but determined to move forward. Whether we stand at the shore because we are just now discovering land, after being lost at sea, or because the fires of the land have pushed us to the shore, and we must swim, here we are, standing at that proverbial, and sometimes literal, boundary between the possible and the seemingly impossible.

New ages and new species are created by courageous souls who stand at the shore without instructions but are willing to utilize the internal and external resources they have, never knowing with certainty if they will succeed or fail—or even what that means.

22

Like any good abusive system, this system has made us dependent upon it. And another important thing about the whole question of abuse is that one of the things that happens within any abusive dynamic, and that's true whether we're talking about an abusive family or an abusive culture,

is that everything—and I mean everything—in this dynamic is set up to
protect the abuser. And so every member of an abusive family comes to
identify more closely with the abuser's feelings than they do their own.
    DERRICK JENSEN

In nearly every book, article, or public appearance, Derrick Jensen compares industrial civilization with an abusive family system. An abusive family system is a closed one, and those who speak the truth about it are scapegoated, castigated, discounted, and, frequently, disowned. Although the so-called democratic West gives lip service to free speech, the unspoken rule is to speak well of one's heritage, one's culture, and one's country—especially in the age of the war on terror.

Nevertheless, industrial civilization is profoundly abusive to its inhabitants and to the earth community. Millions have rebelled against the system and are continuing to rebel, and the second decade of the twenty-first century may well become the age of "occupying" all that is oppressive in industrial civilization. Some claim to have left the abusive system entirely, and while that may still be possible, the harsh reality is that there is virtually nowhere to go to escape the accoutrements of the abuser.

What is also true is that abusers cannot continue to abuse without the assistance of enablers. Many progressives point to "those Republicans" as the perpetrators of abuse, but without the enabling Democrats, the abuse could not continue and would not have reached its current level of severity.

What recourse do we have? While total escape from the abusive system may not be possible, we can extricate ourselves from it to the fullest extent humanly possible. We can, as many readers of this book are doing, choose to live outside the rules of the system, creating our own communities, currencies, food sources, education, health care, childcare, transportation, media, neighborhoods, artistic expression, and spiritual practices. As we do so, however, we will bring with us the emotional baggage of the abusive system; therefore, an essential part of our "leaving" must be our commitment to healing the wounds sustained in the throes of knowingly or unknowingly protecting and perpetuating the abuse.

23

All know that the drop merges into the ocean, but few know that the ocean merges into the drop.

KABIR

In turbulent times we need to be reminded of our intimate connection with the sacred. It is sometimes easier to contemplate ourselves as a drop flowing into the ocean of something greater than it is to imagine the ocean flowing into and merging with us. We can easily understand how we need the sacred but may have more difficulty grasping the extent to which the sacred needs us.

What may be helpful is to contemplate the word *intimate*. Beyond meaning "closely connected," it also means "to commune" and "to make known." When we commune intimately with another person, share deeply what we have in common—whether it be lovemaking or a heart-to-heart conversation—we make ourselves known to the other, and they to us.

When we meditate, contemplate, journal, or pray, we open up to the sacred and make ourselves known. If we listen and remain open, we will be met and responded to, perhaps not in ways we would expect or prefer, but a response *will* occur, and with time and practice, we will gain deeper experiences of something greater. In illogical, mysterious, and nonlinear fashion, we will come to know in our bodies the presence of the sacred, and we will begin to feel—not think—that the ocean is merging into the drop.

Our felt sense of oneness with the sacred as the drop with the ocean and the ocean with the drop is perhaps the greatest spiritual need of our time and, indeed, the supreme antidote to humanity's sense of separation from ourselves, from each other, and from the earth community. Because it is nearly impossible for us to hold this awareness in our bodies and minds permanently, we need to practice experiencing it, and we need to be very patient and merciful with ourselves as we do so. We are as inseparable from the sacred and the sacred from us as the drop from the ocean and the ocean from the drop. As humans, we need practice, but the sacred is already fully present, inextricably connected with us and waiting for us to embrace and savor this intimate communion.

24

What more can we accomplish now than the survival of the soul? Harm and decay are not more present than before, perhaps, only more apparent, more visible and measurable. For the harm which humanity has lived daily since the beginning cannot be increased. But there is increasing insight into humanity's capacity for unspeakable harm, and perhaps where it leads. So much in collapse, so much seeking new ways out. Room for what new can happen.
RAINER MARIA RILKE

It seems that, no matter how much I write and teach that more important than our physical survival is the survival of the soul, some individuals refuse to come to terms with this reality and insist on focusing exclusively on logistical preparation for turbulent times.

Rilke asks, "What more can we accomplish now than the survival of the soul?" He too lived in turbulent times, between the rise to power of Kaiser Wilhelm and the emergence of the Third Reich, with World War I occurring in 1914. Like his contemporary William Butler Yeats, Rilke was deeply disturbed about the trajectory he saw industrial civilization taking. Both Rilke and Yeats understood that millions would become casualties of civilization and that civilization's evils would and could only proliferate, yet both realized that the soul could not be extinguished. Nevertheless, they realized that the soul could waste away as a result of humankind's obsession with power, control, and material acquisition.

We may take issue with Rilke on the issue of the increase of evil in our world, but what matters more is our grasp of the last two sentences of the above quote: *So much in collapse, so much seeking new ways out. Room for what new can happen.*

If the soul is not nurtured and cultivated in preparation for and in the midst of collapse, it will find itself in profound jeopardy amid the chaos, confusion, panic, rage, terror, despair, and nihilism of the masses, who have ignored their souls or perhaps sold them in exchange for the vacuous assurances of industrial civilization. Only by attending diligently to the soul can we make room for all that can happen.

The wondrous moments of our lives should be more frequent than they are in the civilization that we have contrived for ourselves. The comforts of our lives have diminished the wonder. Not only do we miss the dance of life on the planet, but we also fail to see this dance in the universe in which our planet Earth floats—the sun, the stars of the zodiac, the Milky Way galaxy.

THOMAS BERRY, *The Sacred Universe*

Is your life filled with wonder? Is it even possible to experience wonder in times of uncertainty, chaos, and demise? Isn't this a "distraction" from our need to survive?

Granted, these are formidable times, but even as we are navigating massive uncertainties, the stars have not stopped running their courses in the heavens. The sun and moon still appear, even if obscured by humanity's myriad, odious forms of pollution. Many rivers still flow toward the sea; some species of birds still soar and circle in the air.

Stop reading this page for just a moment. Stop right now. Just sit. Take a deep breath and look out the window—or if you are outdoors, look around you. Perhaps you see a tree or the soil beneath your feet or a child at play or an ant crawling on the ground. Take a moment to allow yourself to experience the wonder that is all around you. If you cannot see or be outdoors, allow yourself to remember a time when you were. Remember the wonder of what you saw, touched, smelled, heard, tasted.

Civilization has diminished the wonder, and its collapse opens the doors and windows of wonder once again—the kind of wonder we experienced as children, when we played from dawn until well into the night, then fell exhausted in our beds from dizzying enchantment and total absorption of our senses in it.

Feel the dance of life in your body, on the earth, and in the universe.

26

This is the art of the soul: to harvest your deeper life from all the seasons of your experience.

JOHN O'DONOHUE, *Beauty: The Invisible Embrace*

In his own inimitable way, John O'Donohue once again utilizes one short sentence, poetically proclaimed, to melt the heart and invite the reader toward deep contemplation.

We can also reverse the syntax of the sentence: *to harvest your deeper life from all the seasons of your experience: this is the art of the soul.* The order in which a writer constructs a sentence is significant. In O'Donohue's statement, he puts the art of the soul first, then explains what it is. Clearly, for the late Irish poet, the art of the soul occupied a momentous place in his heart, and defining it was less important to him than actually pondering it.

Yet many of O'Donohue's readers need an explanation, and he has given us a brilliant one in the form of yet another poetic gem: *To harvest your deeper life from all the seasons of your experience.* But what does that really mean?

As we live in times more turbulent and uncertain than most of us have ever experienced, we have entered a new season of life. Indeed, we have entered a season of life that is harsh, unforgiving, volatile, vulnerable, and perhaps even terrifying. Yet O'Donohue would insist that from it there is something to be harvested. Anything harvested is useful, or it wouldn't be harvested. We harvest food crops, animal products, textiles, and natural resources. All are advantageous to us in some way. They help feed, clothe, and provide shelter for us.

What emotional and spiritual harvests are we gathering from the collapse of industrial civilization? O'Donohue asks us not to think in terms of "things" but in terms of our "deeper life." What *is* your deeper life? *Deeper* implies "beneath." What do you know of the life beneath the accoutrements of civilization? What is the value of that life to you? It is all that remains when your physical, human experience is no more.

27

Do you not see how necessary a world of pains and troubles is to school an intelligence and make it a soul?
JOHN KEATS

I am certain of nothing but the holiness of the heart's affections, and the truth of imagination.
JOHN KEATS

The young Romantic poet Keats certainly knew a world of pains and troubles, having lost his parents in childhood, having watched one brother die of tuberculosis and another emigrate to the United States.

In the first statement above, Keats succinctly articulates the process of the intellect being transformed into a soul. How does it happen? Only through experiencing the pains and troubles required to make it so.

When we have opened to the pains and troubles of life and allowed them to school the intelligence, we are then able to say, with Keats, that we are certain of the holiness of the heart's affections and the truth of the imagination.

In these two statements by Keats, we find the essence of the spiritual purpose of this great unraveling for each of us. Some individuals would never be able to grasp anything beyond the intellect were it not for the cataclysmic reverberations of collapse in their lives and psyches.

What constitutes a life well lived? I believe that if one passes from this life and has accomplished nothing more than to utter, with Keats, *I am certain of nothing but the holiness of the heart's affections, and the truth of imagination,* one may have profoundly grasped the meaning of one's existence and thus achieved a life at least partially well lived. Can we allow the pains and troubles of this moment to make it so?

28

It is indeed the mark of a mature adult to be able to carry these two truths simultaneously: Life is hard, filled with loss and suffering. Life is glorious, amazing, stunning, incomparable. To deny either truth is to live in some fantasy of the ideal or to be crushed by the weight of pain. Instead, both are true, and it requires a familiarity with both sorrow and joy to fully encompass the full range of being human.
FRANCIS WELLER, *Entering the Healing Ground: Grief, Ritual, and the Soul of the World*

While there are millions in denial of the collapse of industrial civilization—insisting that civilization is not collapsing or that, if it is, some sort of happy ending will occur—there are many collapse-aware individuals who insist that absolutely nothing positive will result from it and that the unraveling will be unequivocally horrific. I believe that the latter is every bit as delusional as the former.

Paradox is consistent with the underlying principle of evolution, the interplay of opposites: light/dark, cold/hot, masculine/feminine, positive/negative. Weller states above that the capacity to hold the tension of opposites is the mark of a mature individual.

On one occasion, I spoke with someone who believed that the end result of the world crisis would result in nothing positive. He felt contempt for human beings, because of our profligate desecration of the earth and all species on it. In his view, the only positive result of the collapse of industrial civilization would be the opportunity for some species to survive after humans had become extinct. He saw nothing hopeful or transformational coming out of the process. In fact, he argued vehemently for an astonishingly nihilistic outcome. When encountering this perspective, I experience a similar feeling in my body as when I encounter individuals in massive denial of the crisis.

As Weller notes, psychologically, clinging to only one side of the paradox results in either fantasy or grinding despair. Will we become mature adults and choose to hold both instead of one or the other? Will we choose the full range of being human?

29

When we avoid the legitimate suffering that results from dealing with problems, we also avoid the growth that problems demand from us.
SCOTT PECK

Carl Jung asserted that all mental illness is the result of an attempt to avoid legitimate suffering. The tricky word in the statements of Jung and Peck is *legitimate*. Peck clarifies by calling it suffering resulting from dealing with problems.

Buddha tells us that suffering is a fundamental part of the human condition and is exacerbated by attachment to things and to our beliefs in the way life should play out. The human ego believes that we should not have to suffer and that any obstacle in the path toward fulfillment of our desires should be immediately removed. However, to be human is to suffer and to have our desires endlessly thwarted. The ego says, "Adversity, get out of my way and let me have what I want." This is unequivocally an attempt to avoid legitimate suffering.

Just as suffering is inherent in the human condition, the capacity for transformation *through* suffering is inherent in the sacred Self. In fact, when we attempt to avoid adversity, we relinquish the opportunity for transformation that adversity presents to us. Whatever we choose to call it—growth, higher consciousness, or spiritual evolution—each pain, frustration, fear, conflict, disappointment, or loss offers a teaching moment, perhaps many of them.

Our abdication of the opportunity may provide a temporary exit from adversity—or not—but we can be certain that the same or another kind of adversity will appear again and again, offering us yet more opportunities for growth. The paradigm of industrial civilization has convinced us that we are entitled to a life free of suffering. For centuries, humans have bought this bill of goods, and now we are paying the ultimate price: the possibility of our own extinction. The collapse of this paradigm is an extraordinary opportunity to learn, finally and with certainty, how adversity offers itself as a threshold to our personal and collective evolution.

30

Community is that place where the person you least want to live with always lives. And when that person moves away, someone else arises to take his or her place.

PARKER PALMER

Turbulent times will compel many new living arrangements in a world where institutions are crumbling as a result of economic chaos, environmental devastation, and energy depletion. Living alone, "having one's own space," or living with the people we prefer to live with is probably going to become increasingly untenable. More likely in the coming years is the possibility of sharing living space with many people—indeed, many people who are very different from us—in order to survive. This means that, in order to meet our physical needs, we will probably be forced to interact closely with people we do not like, but with whom we will need to learn how to coexist.

The tedious interpersonal processing pervading many intentional communities in current time may become implausible or even unnecessary in communities of the future, driven into existence by the need for cooperation in order to survive. In current time, "getting along" is a luxury we can choose to participate in—or not. In an increasingly chaotic world, our very lives may depend on it.

In community, both in today's world and in the world of the future, we are certain to encounter the people we least want to live with. And as Parker Palmer notes, if we manage to get rid of them, there will always be others to take their place. Thus, it behooves us to learn the skills of deep listening, deep truth telling, and nonviolent communication.

Throughout history, people have been thrown together by wars, revolutions, and both human-caused and natural disasters. In some instances, such groups evolved into workable communities, whereas others devolved into unsustainable hellholes of hostility and competition.

Thus, the sooner we begin preparing to live with those persons we least want to live with, the less surprised we will be when we find ourselves living with them—and the more skillful we may be in doing so.

31

Your profession is not what brings home your paycheck. Your profession is what you were put on earth to do with such passion and such intensity that it becomes spiritual in calling.
VINCENT VAN GOGH

If anyone understood the passion of purpose, it was van Gogh, who perceived the creation of beauty as a sacred calling and who asks us to see our "profession," whatever it may be, with new eyes.

At this moment in history, many people are being forced to reinvent themselves due to the economic collapse that has visited them in the form of loss of employment, bankruptcy, foreclosure, the end of health benefits, and the unwanted downsizing of their lives. This feels most catastrophic for older individuals who have devoted their lives to a career, only to discover that it is over and that they have almost no opportunity for employment that will provide a salary anywhere near the one they have lost.

Younger people find themselves prepared to launch into life after college but quickly discover that it will never be the life they or their parents had planned. Their advantage is that they may be more resilient than the older unemployed, and they may have more options.

Whatever our age and skills, the current unraveling demands that we deeply reevaluate our purpose on earth. Millions of individuals have never considered the questions: What is my purpose in life? What did I come here to do? If the collapse of industrial civilization confronts us with anything, it is these questions. I will push the envelope even further:

Why are you here at this particular time in history? Do you really believe that your presence in the soup of this momentous transformation is accidental?

Consider that you are here at this particular time for specific reasons. Allow yourself to quietly go inside yourself and simply ask the questions: What is my purpose here? What is my work in the world? How can I use my talents and skills to serve the earth community at this time? Where and to whom do I feel drawn to contribute my gifts? Where does my passion lie?

I can assure you that if you ask with a sincere and open heart, sooner or later, you will receive an answer.

32

Wanderer, your footsteps are the road, and nothing more; wanderer, there is no road, the road is made by walking. By walking one makes the road, and upon glancing behind one sees the path that never will be trod again. Wanderer, there is no road—Only wakes upon the sea.
ANTONIO MACHADO

Because there has never before been a collapse of industrial civilization, no one knows how to navigate it well. Countless civilizations throughout human history have collapsed, however, and we can learn from their former inhabitants. If they could speak to us today, they would no doubt tell us what Machado is saying: *Your footsteps are the road; there is no road, the road is made by walking.*

In recent years we have had the privilege of reading and listening to Dmitry Orlov speak very frankly about the collapse of the Soviet Union. For me, Orlov's words have been comforting, terrifying, inspiring, and, at times, hysterically funny. Nevertheless, like other accounts of collapsing civilizations or countries, his stories of the demise of the Soviet Union and how people responded echo the words of Machado. People navigated by navigating. The road was made by walking.

Those who survive this enormous transition and are responsible for creating a next culture will invariably feel overwhelmed by the task. They will be able to tell the rest of the world much about how they navigated the demise, and that will inform the kind of world they construct going forward. They may find themselves on a planet largely uninhabitable, with vast numbers of species made extinct, including millions of humans obliterated. We have nothing in human history to compare with how confounded these individuals will feel.

They will *glance behind and see the path that never will be trod again.* Some of what they see will be useful in creating the next culture; some of it will not be. But regardless of what they see from hindsight or how flabbergasted they feel, they will discover that *by walking, one makes the road.*

33

I wish I could show you when you are lonely or in darkness the astonishing light of your own being.
    HAFIZ

How often have we felt this longing when we see someone we care about sitting in suffering and pain? We long for our loved one to draw on his or her incalculable inner resources and utilize them to move through the darkness. But when *we* are slogging through a time of anguish, we may not be as easily moved by these words of Hafiz.

Darkness can feel overpowering, overwhelming; it can make us feel as if we will never see light again. Worse, in the midst of it, we can be convinced that the light in which we basked in former times was an illusion or even a cosmic joke.

Living in a world in decline sometimes feels this way, and we need to fortify ourselves for times when we may feel that we will never again experience the light. We do not do this by attempting to shut out the darkness—deny it, ignore it, or minimize it. We cannot *make* the light return or the darkness subside. Rather, we hold the light and darkness together in our bodies and souls.

If we are struggling with loss, we acknowledge it and deal with it pragmatically. At the same time, we give thanks for what we still have. If we are in danger, we protect ourselves and acknowledge our ability to do so. As with any cloudy day, the light has not been extinguished; it is only obscured by overcast skies.

There is a particular tenderness with which Hafiz speaks the above words. I've found that when I simply sit quietly with them and repeat them to myself, something shifts. I feel the exquisite softness of a nurturing mother in this utterance. As is so often the case with a poet's words, the way in which they are spoken is as momentous as their meaning. Feel Hafiz reaching out to you—or, rather, into your heart. Feel his heart longing to help you remember the astonishing light of your own being. Feel how much he wants that for you, and then notice what happens in your body. Ah, yes, feel it. And when you do, know that you have just rediscovered the light that cannot be extinguished but can only be obscured for a time.

It is no accident that we've been born in these times, that we find our lives unfolding now, with our particular histories and gifts, our brokenness, our experience, and our wisdom. It is not an accident.
MIRIAM MACGILLIS, *Genesis Farm*

I'm fond of telling people that they did not just fall out of the sky in the twentieth or twenty-first century and land on this troubled planet.

Whether or not we believe in past lives or reincarnation or any existence after this one, it is likely that we sometimes wonder why we were born in this time. Even if the thought has never crossed our minds, the question is compelling, as we look around at a world in chaos and collapse.

When contemplating this question, it is easy for the ego to assume that we are here because we have particular gifts to offer, yet Miriam MacGillis includes "our brokenness" as part of the contribution our presence here makes. We are not likely to be stymied when asking, what do our histories, gifts, experience, and wisdom offer these turbulent times but our brokenness?

We are all wounded souls, but what good are our wounds in a world unraveling, already so abysmally wounded?

For me, this is a riveting question. What can my wounds offer the world?

Whatever our wounds—growing up in an abusive family, suffering from post-traumatic stress, addictions, depression, self-loathing, self-absorption, cynicism, bitterness, envy, despair—all of the demons with which we currently struggle or have struggled in the past. How can the world benefit from them?

I cannot answer this question for you, dear reader, because I am grappling with answering it for myself. Yet I believe it is a momentous question, one that each of us needs to confront. We spend so much time running from our brokenness, but in reality, we need it, and it needs us—and so does our shattered world.

35

Getting older by itself does not cause us to mature psychologically. Adolescence is not at all confined to our teen years. And adulthood cannot be meaningfully defined as what happens in our twenties or when we fulfill certain responsibilities, such as holding down a job, financial independence, or raising a family. Rather, an adult is someone who understands

*why he is here on Earth, why he was born, and is offering his unique
contribution to the more-than-human world.*

BILL PLOTKIN

As we ponder the question, *what is collapse asking from me and from my
species?* we must consider that any demise confronts us with choices,
and choices can only be meaningfully made by adults. Older children may
be given minimal choices on the road to maturity, but much of adult functioning consists of making consequential choices on a daily basis.

Unlike indigenous cultures or cultures historically eviscerated by
war, famine, and natural disasters, industrialized cultures, most notably
American culture, are both chronologically young and young in terms of
suffering. Industrial civilization is profoundly growth stunting. Its inhabitants are encouraged to focus on material acquisition, ego satisfaction,
and power. In order to achieve some semblance of maturity of the kind
described by Bill Plotkin, most of us must "grow ourselves up," by way of
navigating the numerous initiations and ordeals life presents to us. Conscious work with our emotions and a commitment to a spiritual path are
essential tools in understanding why we are here and why we were born
and in discerning what unique contributions we can make to the earth
community.

Collapse is not only asking that we grow up, it is compelling us to do
so. Ask people in their fifties who suddenly lost their jobs, after decades
of engagement in a successful career, what now really matters to them.
Some may answer that they are still pursuing work in their field, but even
those folks will admit that they have been forced—on a deeper level than
they ever imagined—to consider the meaning and purpose of their lives.
In other words, they are being compelled to "grow themselves up," which
has much less to do with what kind of job one does and much more to do
with contemplating why one is moving and breathing on planet earth in
the twenty-first century.

36

The time before was one in which we insisted and relied on hope, on bet-ter tomorrows, in the United States on the "American Dream." Now, we have to accept that "better tomorrows" may not come. It is akin to accept-ing one's own mortality, maybe a doctor's prognosis of one's impending death, but on a much grander scale.

        SUSANNE MOSER, "Getting Real about It: Meeting the Psychological and Social Demands of a World in Distress"

In the first decade of the twenty-first century, we often hear the support-ive maxim, "It gets better." Usually this is directed to victims of some type of exploitation or discrimination, with an eye to encouraging them to persevere and not give up. Americans are doggedly and unrealistically optimistic, and this is different from holding a positive vision in the face of adversity. One can hold a positive vision of what could be possible even when the opposite overwhelmingly prevails.

The optimism of the American Dream, which implacably believes that not only *will* things get better, but that, as Americans, we are entitled to their getting better, is now being confronted by the irrefutable reali-ties of global economic meltdown, climate change, and energy depletion. Despite glowing stock market numbers and jobs reports, most middle-class Americans know in their bones that things aren't getting better and never will. They have a gut-feeling awareness that "brighter tomorrows" are over forever.

Culturally and personally, this is absolutely akin to accepting one's own mortality. For this reason, working with our own mortality, as I do in many of my workshops, where I facilitate a "die before you die" exercise, is extremely useful in assisting people in experiencing that their death is not the worst thing that could happen to them.

As asserted by many of the great wisdom traditions, the death of the soul is far more wrenching than the death of the body. Our souls begin to die when we ward off all those challenges that could deepen them, as the collapse of industrial civilization has the potential to do. The soul is fed by descent into the darkness of loss, poverty, uncertainty, and ego death. Likewise, the soul atrophies when we defend against the ordeals that feed, expand, nurture, and cultivate it. The soul of Western culture is dying, but we can prevent the death of our individual souls by consciously surrendering to the disappearance of "better tomorrows."

37

Who ever got the idea that we could have pleasure without pain? . . . Pain and pleasure go together; they are inseparable. They can be celebrated. They are ordinary. Birth is painful and delightful. Death is painful and delightful. . . . Pain is not punishment, pleasure is not a reward. Inspiration and wretchedness are inseparable. We always want to get rid of misery rather than see how it works together with joy.
PEMA CHÖDRÖN

The culture of industrial civilization is inherently dualistic, splitting pain and pleasure into opposites. Moreover, we are socialized to believe that pleasure is good and pain is bad and that we should strive to maintain a state of pleasure for as long as possible and minimize the duration of our pain. Under the influence of organized religion, we have also come to believe that pain is a punishment and pleasure is a reward.

The Eastern spiritual tradition, however, teaches the oneness of all things, reminding us that so-called opposites need each other and mysteriously work together at different times for different purposes. For the Western mind, the notion that pain and pleasure are different parts of one whole is foreign and, at times, inconceivable. Entertaining this possibility, however, and living from this perspective not only decreases our stress but alleviates our knee-jerk tendency to judge what is happening as "good" or "bad."

I believe that the dissolution of the old paradigm will provide an opportunity to discover the value of pain and reevaluate what the culture of empire has offered us as "pleasurable." It will provide new opportunities to explore the polarization of pain and pleasure and to experience in our own bodies the ways in which these two concepts are inextricably connected, rather than terminally antithetical to each other.

The pain of collapse may be tempered by myriad epiphanies along the way that will reveal how distorted our notions of "pain" and "pleasure" have become and the extent to which the anguish of loss is a prerequisite for the joy inherent in a new paradigm. As we learn to hold pain and pleasure together in the body and in consciousness, we increase the likelihood that a third option may arise that transcends the so-called opposites and transforms both us and the external situation.

38

If you ask me what I came into this life to do, I will tell you: I came to live out loud.
  ÉMILE ZOLA

Émile Zola, a French novelist of the nineteenth century, was willing to risk his life to speak out on behalf of justice and ordinary human beings. Perhaps no other historical figure has given us a clearer or more concise statement of life purpose than these words from Zola.

But what does it mean to "live out loud"? Does it mean that we are constantly verbalizing our perceptions? Incessantly writing articles or blogging? Does it mean being disruptive, getting arrested, playing the role of gadfly in a numbed-out world? It could mean all of these, but I believe living out loud means much more than these.

First, living out loud means having a clear sense of purpose about what you came here to do, as Zola so brazenly declares for himself. One of the subtle and perhaps unwanted gifts of an unraveling society is that many individuals will be dramatically confronted with questions of meaning and purpose. As a result, they will be compelled to address how they want to live their lives—as well as what gifts they want to share—in a chaotic world.

Living out loud means that you begin *now* to explore and define your purpose—what it is you came here to do. Quite naturally, as a result of that exploration, you discern how you can utilize your gifts and live them out loud. You may do all of this in very quiet ways but perhaps with an impact that reverberates through the lives of many suffering humans or other members of the earth community.

None of us really has any idea how many lives we touch or what impact we have on those lives. In most cases, we will never get to see what difference we made, but living out loud isn't about noticing the results. It is about doing what we came here to do, for no reason other than that it is our life purpose.

39

It's only when we truly know and understand that we have a limited time on earth—and that we have no way of knowing when our time is up— that we will begin to live each day to the fullest, as if it were the only one we had.

ELISABETH KÜBLER-ROSS

From the heart of one of the most notable researchers of death comes this momentous statement, which, it seems to me, is a wonderful maxim for all "elders of collapse" to live by.

In a world in which state-of-the-art medicine, nutrition, and fitness have extended life spans to an unprecedented extent, we are now facing diminishing access to health care; skyrocketing levels of toxins in our air, food, and water; the threat of rapidly mutating viruses that resist antibiotics; worldwide shortages of vital medications; and ever-spiraling rates of cancer. Health care is inexorably going to be one of the most dramatic casualties of the demise of industrial civilization, and it's anyone's guess just how widespread and severe the death of health care as we know it will become. What is certain is that, as modern medicine goes away, so will the extended life spans to which we have become accustomed.

Throughout my work, I have suggested mindfulness practices for working with one's own death. Here I would reiterate that suggestion and add, as I have stated many times in this book and elsewhere, that physical survival of collapse is not the endgame. In fact, I suspect that few reading these words will endure until collapse has evolved into the next culture. Thus, one half of our collapse preparation should be preparation for death, as well as preparation for survival.

Live each day to the fullest, and prepare not only your internal and external bunker but the legacy you plan to leave for those who will carry on when you are no longer here.

40

Morning has broken, like the first morning
Blackbird has spoken, like the first bird
Praise for the singing, praise for the morning
Praise for them springing fresh from the Word.
ELEANOR FARJEON

"Morning Has Broken," a hymn published in 1931 by a British author of children's books, speaks as powerfully to us in the twenty-first century as it did in the 1930s and as it did in the 1970s, when it was recorded and made into a classic by Cat Stevens. Whether we apply the words to the beginning of a new twenty-four-hour day or the dawn of a new era of human consciousness, the beauty and poignancy of the song are the same.

I sometimes begin a new day by singing the song aloud or in my mind as I stand on the threshold of another segment of my life between sunrise and sunset. I invite you to ponder and memorize the words and sing the song at the beginning of the day, at the beginning of a new endeavor, or whenever you feel that you have encountered a final loss. It is both a song of gratitude and of affirmation that while every ending is a loss, it is also an extraordinary new beginning.

41

The place you are right now God circled on a map for you.
HAFIZ

> *The poet tells you*
> *god has put a circle around you on a map*
> *To locate you in sacred space.*
> *Then why do you keep tunneling underground,*
> *Carving labyrinths for your escape?*
> DOROTHY WALTERS, *Marrow of Flame: Poems of the*
> *Spiritual Journey*

On some level, we all want to escape from turbulent times. Most of us remember how easy it used to be—to find a job, to buy or sell a home, to get a good college education for cheap, to have full health care coverage, to save money, to take summer vacations, and to just live our lives. Of course, much of the ease of our lives was acquired at the expense of earth's resources and resulted in the slaughter of countless members of the more-than-human world. As a result, our lives today are becoming increasingly difficult to manage, and for many who once lived comfortably, having enough to eat, securing a roof over their heads at night, finding access to any health care at all, acquiring meaningful employment, or connecting with companions with whom to share their struggles is only a fleeting fantasy. Perhaps this last sentence describes your life—or the life you are terrified you may be forced to live.

While I do not wish to romanticize this kind of existence or imply that the reader should just grin and bear it, because it's "happening for a reason," I do suggest that wherever we are, we are in the middle of a circle drawn for us by life. We may never know the reason, or the reason may be revealed over time. Either way, we are likely to discover that our situation inside the circle makes more sense if we can open to the possibility that it was drawn for us by something greater than mental reasoning. Alongside that "sense," we may also discover some contentment that could elude us if we persist in attempting to dig our way out.

42

Since we humans are ourselves part of nature, we have an ancient wisdom and wildness in ourselves that we can tap into—if only we slow down and are mindful enough to do so. Tapping into our soul—the core of each of us that is both inside and outside us and that holds our ancient animal wisdom—is done through various means of internalizing nature. Internalizing nature means having it be part of who we are, not just something we use for our personal benefit.

MARGARET EMERSON, *Contemplative Hiking along the Colorado Front Range*

When was the last time you tapped into your wildness? If you have no clue what that even means, it's time to find out. The best way to do so is to spend time—and I mean *quality* time—in nature. In order to do so, you must slow down, and you must remember that after a lifetime of being estranged from nature, it takes weeks, months, even years to develop the kind of relationship with nature that Margaret Emerson is talking about.

You see, when you immerse yourself in nature's wildness, beauty, bounty, uncertainty, capriciousness, innocence, treachery, and—yes—love, you will be changed. I don't know how, I only know that you will be. I also know that spending contemplative time in nature will invariably cause you to take some or all of that time with you, back into your everyday world, and that will inevitably change how you live it. It means "having it be part of who we are."

What would it be like to have nature become part of who you are? Perhaps you already know because you have been spending quality time in it for many years, or perhaps you have no idea who you would be if nature were part of you. And even if you have already discovered the answer to the question, the answers never cease. That is to say that even after years of living constantly in nature, some people continue to be surprised by how they are made and remade by it.

No one can predict how internalizing nature will affect him, but once it has, nothing will ever be the same.

43

Our sorrow eases the hardened places within us, allowing them to open again and freeing us to once more feel our kinship with the living presence around us. This is deep activism, soul activism that actually encourages us to connect with the tears of the world.
          FRANCIS WELLER, *Entering the Healing Ground:*
          Grief, Ritual, and the Soul of the World

In the days following September 11, 2001, many communities in the United States, particularly in the New York City region, were in a state of profound mourning. For the first time since perhaps the end of World War II, Americans experienced a palpable kinship with each other. Hearts were softened and opened. Yes, some people immediately "suited up" for war, but many more constructed altars and memorial walls and held rituals that facilitated deep grief. Many wanted to take action; many were stunned and compelled to simply feel.

From my perspective, feeling and acting should not be polarized, yet in this culture, the person who follows the magnetic pull of emotion to the soul's true north and allows himself to grieve is sometimes accused of inaction. Conversely, the person who shunts or denies her grief in favor of taking action is perceived as responsive, inspired, and passionate. Activists are supposed to *act,* not grieve.

Yet I want to ask: What might happen if activists regularly allowed themselves to grieve? What if the injustices that enrage them were grieved as well as acted upon? I ask because my experience has been that when people allow themselves to fully grieve their losses, they almost always want to take action. They become activists or in some way make a difference in their world. They also recognize that some grief never ends, and they allow themselves to keep descending into ever-circling, ever-deepening layers of loss.

Grieving together connects us intimately with each other and with the world. We are forever changed by connecting with the tears of the world, and who knows to what extent the tears of the world are influenced by our grieving. Grieving facilitates true kinship—with our own and with the more-than-human world. We have a responsibility to grieve; in fact, I would argue that it is part of our civic and cosmic duty, because it may be the purest form of activism—the activism of the soul.

44

Asking the proper question is the central act of transformation.
CLARISSA PINKOLA ESTÉS

In these turbulent times, one of the things I find most appalling is the seeming inability of humans to ask proper questions. For example, mainstream media reports about any sort of tragedy are often followed by the question, "Who's to blame?" or "What did they know and when did they know it?"

At this writing, in 2012, much of the United States is engulfed in a ghastly heat wave that has broken over 4,500 records across the nation. In the midst of this inferno, President Obama spoke at an outdoor gathering in Pennsylvania. The temperature was 106 degrees, and twenty-five people passed out from the heat, yet not once during his speech did Obama refer to global warming or climate change.

Because industrial civilization is a paradigm of avarice operating in conjunction with avoidance, its inhabitants, for the most part, do not learn to ask astute or incisive questions that penetrate its vacuous assumptions. Rather, they are socialized to become myopic, obtuse, and psychically numb.

What would happen to humanity if we began asking questions like the following? What does a whale experience as a result of oil drilling in the Arctic? How does she become disoriented, deaf, and eventually dead as a result? Why are we not willing to radically alter our lifestyles in order to simplify them and, therefore, use vastly less energy? What terrifies us about doing so? Is there more to life than shopping, eating, accumulating debt, having children, and living out the American or some other dream?

Collapse is forcing and will continue to force humans to ask questions they should have asked decades ago but could not or would not, because they were muddling through life under the influence of the soporific of civilization. When we begin struggling to find the proper questions instead of answers to superficial ones, we will be able to access clearer paths to viable options for our dilemmas. Our search for solutions must follow the trajectory of penetrating, disturbing, life-altering questions if we are to create a new culture that radically departs from this one.

45

Beauty and grace are performed whether or not we will or sense them. The least we can do is be there.

ANNIE DILLARD

So many aspects of the universe have a life of their own. Often it seems that tragedy and suffering are relentless energies that insist on revisiting us without any respite. It may be that these energies do have a life of their own, but if that is so, perhaps it is also true that beauty and grace have lives of their own.

The old paradigm says that if we are devoutly religious, we can mitigate the possibility of bad things happening to us. This worldview says that we can somehow insulate ourselves from adversity through practicing our piety. The ancients did not subscribe to this notion. Rather, they believed that the multifarious energies of the universe all have lives of their own and that it is our responsibility to be open to the sacred and understand that we have no idea what energies will visit us next. While native peoples often construct rituals or carry sacred objects that they believe will help protect them from adversity, they know well that suffering is a fact of life and that all adversity has the potential to increase meaning and purpose in our lives.

In ancient and indigenous traditions, one's responsibility is to show up in relationship with the sacred and see what arises. This does not guarantee any particular response from the sacred. We do not show up in order to control or appease the mystery, we simply show up with awe and reverence for it. If we honor *all* of the myriad energies of the universe, we must also know that beauty and grace appear in our lives as often as suffering.

There are fundamental questions here: Are we present for the eruption of beauty and grace in our lives, as well as the eruption of suffering? Are we truly available for whatever energies manifest? Some would argue that the universe is "conspiring in our favor." I personally have great difficulty with the notion that the universe is "conspiring" to do anything in relation to me or my life. Life happens to all of us. Are we present to celebrate and give thanks for outpourings of grace and beauty, and are we equally present to be remade by their most daunting opposites?

46

What has no shadow has no strength of life.
CZESŁAW MIŁOSZ

But if we are able to see our own shadow and can bear knowing about it, then a small part of the problem has already been solved.
CARL JUNG

Look for your other half who walks always next to you and tends to be who you aren't.
ANTONIO MACHADO

Somewhere in the process of industrial civilization's demise, humans will be forced to confront the shadow. Many are already doing so, as they allow themselves to learn about and process the consequences of humanity's shadow that has been unleashed upon the earth community for the past three centuries. Confronting the shadow within oneself and one's culture is difficult and painful work.

The shadow is all that we say is "not me," all that we deny. What are we denying or avoiding when, speaking of ourselves, we say "I am a good and decent human being," or speaking of our nation, "This is the greatest country in the world." We may be a decent human being, but what lies in the shadow of our decency?

What do you know about your shadow? What parts of yourself do you disown? What qualities in others "push your buttons"? Know that those qualities reside in your shadow. Deep shadow work involves claiming those qualities and noticing how they manifest in your life.

Jung suggested dialoging with the shadow. This can be done in a meditative or contemplative state by speaking directly with the shadow and asking it what it wants from us. We can also explore the shadow through our creative works—art, music, writing—and noticing what we discover. Jung believed that much of the shadow is, in his words, "pure gold," because of the life-force energy it provides. Get to know your shadow and what it offers you. After all, it *is* your other half.

47

Spiritual growth is now replacing survival as the central objective of the human experience.
GARY ZUKAV AND LINDA FRANCIS, *The Heart of the Soul*

Industrial civilization has been all about survival, and even as many people prepare for the collapse of it, their focus is on survival only. In all of my writing and speaking about collapse, I emphasize that many of us, perhaps most of us, may not survive it. We have created a plethora of "extinction events," which may also include our own.

I believe that it is futile and a waste of precious life-force energy to focus exclusively on the survival aspect of collapse. I support people in preparing logistically as they much as they can, but I am cautious about suggesting that this is enough—because it isn't. Due to the likelihood that many of us may not survive collapse, something else must be at the core of our preparation for it. Just reading the words on this page automatically catapults you into the territory of mystery, that is, the sacred. And quite frankly, that is where I hope you will be, because that is where you *need* to be as we face the demise of the old paradigm.

Natural disasters often motivate people to seek or deepen their spiritual path. They may do so for a while, then return to their malaise with regard to the sacred after the hurricane or drought has passed. But collapse is not an event; it's a process, and one that is likely to last a very long time.

Within that process may occur many events that feel like serial natural disasters. It will be nerve-wracking and traumatic, to say the least. It will push every button in our bodies, and some people may not be able to endure. We can expect many emotional breakdowns and suicides. Yet I hasten to add that collapse will not play out identically in every place. Some places will be far more stressed than others.

Regardless of how collapse plays out, what will almost certainly result is a new emphasis on the sacred, with many individuals plumbing the depths of the soul and discovering treasures there that they never knew existed. This is not to imply that survival will no longer be important, but survival is likely to find its rightful place in our psyches, not as the most important instinct, but as one of many others—many of which have to do with something greater within us than the rational mind and the human ego.

How important it is that we learn the sacred story of our evolutionary Universe, just as we have learned our cultural and religious stories. Each day we will do what humans do best: Be amazed! Be filled with reverence! Contemplate! Fall in love! Be entranced by the wonder of the Universe, the willingness of each being, the beauty of Creation, its new revelation each day, and the Divine Presence with all!

MARY SOUTHARD

Mary Southard is a Roman Catholic Sister of St. Joseph and a phenomenal artist. Her life and work can be found at her website (www.marysouthardart.org). She is one of many who have discovered, through spiritual teachers such as Thomas Berry, what they now refer to as the "story of the universe."

Twentieth-century French paleontologist and Jesuit priest, Teilhard de Chardin, departed from some Roman Catholic traditions when he penned

The Phenomenon of Man, in which he argued that humans are part of the universe and that spirit dwells within both matter and human beings. His teachings deeply influenced Father Thomas Berry in the United States, who began writing and teaching the "story of the universe." If we do not know the story of the universe, we do not know ourselves. In fact, we do not know anything.

Berry spent ten years collaborating with mathematical cosmologist, Dr. Brian Swimme, who founded the Center for the Story of the Universe in Northern California. Swimme and Berry argue that the story of the universe is our story, the human story, the story of life in the universe contained in one sacred whole. They also assert that one of the reasons humans have so tragically devastated our ecosystems is that we do not know our story or understand the extent to which we are connected with the universe.

Mary Southard passionately proclaims that when we understand the story of the universe and our part in it, we will be profoundly amazed, filled with reverence, and will both fall in love with and fall at the feet of our earth in wonder and gratitude. According to Mary, when we fully understand our part in the story, we are compelled to create in some fashion. Visual arts, music, writing, storytelling, or sacred spaces, or even offspring, we cannot help but create when we are infused with the universe's story, our story—the story that makes the universe and our lives make sense.

49

The cure for despair is not hope. It's discovering what we want to do about something we care about.
MARGARET WHEATLEY

In the era of the Obama presidency in the United States, we have heard much about "hope." In fact, this word proved phenomenally useful in catapulting Obama to success as a presidential candidate in 2008. He wrote a book entitled *The Audacity of Hope* and sold his campaign as an agenda of hope for "change we can believe in."

Today, in 2012, the American people feel perhaps more hopeless than ever, as global economic meltdown, energy depletion, and environmental degradation are closing in from every side. What is needed now is not another marketing campaign based on hope, but clear, decisive action informed by the realities of the collapse of industrial civilization. The political process of nearly every country on earth is unraveling, alongside all of the other institutions of those nations. The action we need to take is not about rearranging deck chairs on the Titanic or tidying up catastrophic train wrecks. Rather, humans need to understand collapse and all of its ramifications and prepare themselves logistically, emotionally, and spiritually as quickly and as thoroughly as possible.

This does not mean that we should abandon efforts to improve our individual lives and communities. In fact, part of our preparation for the dissolution of life as we have known it should be implementing new systems and working to keep those intact as the larger project of civilization disintegrates. For example, having a local food system or an alternative currency or bartering system in place may alleviate much of the shock and suffering of total collapse.

Emphasis on "hope" guarantees a high degree of passivity and is based on an assumption that hope comes from something outside of us. In my experience, this leads only to further despair. Rather, taking intelligent action in response to an astute understanding of our predicament is empowering and increases the likelihood of survival. As a result, despair has no place to germinate and grow.

50

Where you come from is gone, where you thought you were going to never was there, and where you are is no good unless you can get away from it.

Where is there a place for you to be? No place. . . . In yourself right now is all the place you've got.

FLANNERY O'CONNOR, *Wise Blood*

In the culture of industrial civilization, the individual carries the day. We pay lip service to community, but in reality, only remnants of one exist—and less so with every passing day. As we awaken to the travesty that is the old paradigm and work to create a new one, we feel the loss of community and long for the social safety nets that have been the fabric of so many Western countries, but are now in tatters. Realizing the consequences of what we have lost, it is easy to become engulfed in a new-found community, if we can find one or form one, while minimizing our individual needs. For most of us, the collapse of industrial civilization will challenge us to feel our way toward a balance between individuality and community.

Such was the tension that haunted the psyche of American novelist Flannery O'Connor, whose novel *Wise Blood* was replete with characters who depicted this tension brilliantly. O'Connor's bias was on the side of individual experiences of piety and against religious dogma that facilitated a kind of groupthink.

As we navigate collapse, a useful motto might be, "In yourself right now is all the place you've got." On the other hand, it may feel like community is the only place we've got. In fact, both are true. If we are fortunate enough to be held in a caring community, we must cherish it dearly, yet never banish our individual needs entirely. Inside ourselves is still the only place we've got. If we are not living in community, and if we are more often alone than joined with others, then O'Connor's words are all the more timely.

More importantly, the inside place, while it may be disorienting and mysterious, is the domain of the deeper Self. The deeper Self cannot be accessed unless we are willing to abide with the "no place" that we often feel when we turn our attention inward in order to access the deeper Self.

When we do access it, we are likely to discover that it is our true north, our true home, our true place in all that was and never will be again.

51

The question is whether any civilization can wage relentless war on life without destroying itself, and without losing the right to be called civilized.

RACHEL CARSON

A chorus of voices that previously rejected the reality of climate change is now coming forth to support the hard science that verifies unequivocally that humans are altering the chemistry of the earth and the ecosystems. The mainstream media is currently reporting the authenticity of climate change and the recognition by former climate change deniers that it has been unfolding for decades. Whatever their motivation, a significant number of climate skeptics are jumping ship and recognizing the frightening ramifications of global warming.

At the same time, humanity is frantically engaged in acquiring more fossil fuel energy by any means necessary. In the face of staggering droughts around the world, humanity displays its mad, implacable insistence on maintaining its profligate lifestyle by utilizing practices such as hydraulic fracturing and coal and nuclear power—all of which place ghastly demands on fresh water supplies. Droughts have created mega-crises in the food and water supply, yet even in the face of starvation and thirst, inhabitants of civilization demand not only the continuation of their lifestyle but an augmentation of it. Can this be called anything but mental illness?

One of the first environmentalists in the modern world, Rachel Carson suggests that when we wage this kind of war on the earth community, we lose our right to be called "civilized." Of course, Carson viewed *civilized* as a favorable term. With all we have discovered about industrial civilization and where it has taken us since she wrote *Silent Spring* in 1962, we now understand that calling ourselves "civilized" is hardly a flattering assessment of who we are.

If you are reading these words, hopefully, you are happy to be labeled "uncivilized," because you understand that civilization is destroying itself and everything in its wake. In fact, civilization, by definition, is incapable of doing otherwise. Rather than being civilized, is it not more congruent with our humanity to be "harmonized" with the earth community—to ask the earth what it wants from us and to live accordingly?

52

WHY I AM HAPPY

Now has come, an easy time. I let it
roll. There is a lake somewhere
so blue and far nobody owns it . . .
That lake stays blue and free; it goes
on and on.

And I know where it is.

WILLIAM STAFFORD

Ever writing from depths far more subtle than meets the eye, William Stafford speaks of both his laugh and cry for the world in its innocent spin. Even as he revels in the deep, blue, peaceful lake, he is not oblivious to the suffering of the world. But implicit in his words is the suggestion that he can endure the planet's anguish because the lake stays free and blue and goes on and on.

Stafford alludes to the depth and tranquility of a lake somewhere. The picture he paints is entirely placid and free of sorrow. Characteristically

Stafford, the poem was probably inspired by an actual experience in nature, which he utilizes to evoke a deeper awareness in the reader of her inner world.

The poet is happy not merely because of a serene lake that he has access to, even as he reflects on humanity's angst. The awesome significance of this poem is in the line, "I know where it is." Holding both opposites in this deceivingly simple poem, Stafford invites us to remember the stillness within each of us. It's free and blue and goes on and on, but most importantly, each of us knows where it is. Your work—our work—is to access the stillness many times a day and recognize that, regardless of what happens externally, that stillness remains. It can never be taken away from us. It is always there, and it goes on and on.

CONSTANT

We live for constants,
rain in winter, the cat
curled like a furry comma
on the edge of the bed.

Sometimes, many times
these don't come, instead
there is drought, the father dies,
the mother grows old.

The constant is this:
the mind insists, persists in the insane
circle of creation from chaos.
Make order of mystery.

"Listen to me," it shouts.
So we listen.
Constant chatter, constant need
growing like a curse.

The constant is this:
life is chaos, disintegration, blooming
anew into order and collapsing
again to blossom into something more perfect,
then chaos, disintegration and on.

We watch helplessly, entranced
like the magician's audience,
the hypnotist's mark.

Nothing to do but join hands,
bow heads, say blessings
to the capricious, wild
original god.

REBECCA DEL RIO

About the Author

Carolyn Baker, PhD, is a former psychotherapist and professor of psychology and history. She is nationally renowned for her writing and workshops on emotional resilience in challenging times, as well as for life coaching for individuals and groups. Her books include *Navigating the Coming Chaos: A Handbook for Inner Transition* and *Sacred Demise: Walking the Spiritual Path of Industrial Civilization's Collapse*. She lives and writes in Boulder, Colorado. Her website is Speaking Truth to Power, at www.carolynbaker.net.

Heart in Action

Sacred Activism Series Titles

When the joy of compassionate service is combined with the pragmatic drive to transform all existing economic, social, and political institutions, a radical divine force is born: Sacred Activism. The Sacred Activism Series, published by North Atlantic Books, presents leading voices that embody the tenets of Sacred Activism—compassion, service, and sacred consciousness—while addressing the crucial issues of our time and inspiring radical action.

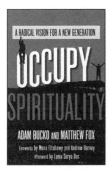  

Occupy Spirituality
Adam Bucko and
Matthew Fox

The More Beautiful World
Our Hearts Know Is Possible
Charles Eisenstein

Earth Calling
Ellen Gunter
and Ted Carter
APRIL, 2014

The Sacred Activism Series was cocreated by Andrew Harvey, visionary, spiritual teacher and founder of the Institute for Sacred Activism, and Douglas Reil, associate publisher and managing director of North Atlantic Books. Harvey serves as the series editor and drives outreach efforts worldwide.

For more information about the Sacred Activism series, go to:
www.nabcommunities.com/sacredactivism

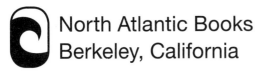

North Atlantic Books
Berkeley, California

Personal, spiritual, and planetary transformation

North Atlantic Books, a nonprofit publisher established in 1974, is dedicated to fostering community, education, and constructive dialogue. NABCommunities.com is a meeting place for an ever-growing membership of readers and authors to engage in the discussion of books and topics from North Atlantic's core publishing categories.

NAB Communities offer interactive social networks in these genres:

NOURISH: Raw Foods, Healthy Eating and Nutrition, All-Natural Recipes

WELLNESS: Holistic Health, Bodywork, Healing Therapies

WISDOM: New Consciousness, Spirituality, Self-Improvement

CULTURE: Literary Arts, Social Sciences, Lifestyle

BLUE SNAKE: Martial Arts History, Fighting Philosophy, Technique

Your free membership gives you access to:

Advance notice about new titles and exclusive giveaways

Podcasts, webinars, and events

Discussion forums

Polls, quizzes, and more!

Go to www.NABCommunities.com and join today.